FORTY CRAZY YEARS
of
Friendship

Richard Hulse

FORTY CRAZY YEARS OF FRIENDSHIP

iUniverse books may be ordered through booksellers or by contacting:

iUniverse
1663 Liberty Drive
Bloomington, IN 47403
www.iuniverse.com
1-800-Authors (1-800-288-4677)

Because of the dynamic nature of the Internet, any web
addresses or links contained in this book may have changed
since publication and may no longer be valid. The views
expressed in this work are solely those of the author and do
not necessarily reflect the views of the publisher, and the
publisher hereby disclaims any responsibility for them.

Any people depicted in stock imagery provided by Thinkstock are
models, and such images are being used for illustrative purposes only.
Certain stock imagery © Thinkstock.

ISBN: 978-1-4917-7037-5 (sc)
ISBN: 978-1-4917-7038-2 (e)

Library of Congress Control Number: 2015909476

Print information available on the last page.

iUniverse rev. date: 06/29/2015

the story are based on conversations with friends and relatives, my personal experiences and recollections, and my notes and writings.

I wish to thank my wife, Debi, who provided me with meaningful support, served as my editor, and provided constructive criticism as she helped me develop the story.

Preface

I spoke to my friend, Baines Spivington, the night before he passed away. I had no idea it would be the last time we would speak to one another, and our crazy, forty year friendship would come to a tragic abrupt end.

The following is a true story about the life of my friend. It is based on facts and actual events that occurred in his life. The dialogue is as accurate as I can recall. In this work of narrative nonfiction, I have reimagined some of the scenes or reconstructed events in a way I believe reflects the essence of the scenes or events in the minds and hearts of the people who lived through them.

This is meant to be a memorial to the life of my friend, Baines Spivington. His life was not boring, and during much of his life, he avoided or leaned away from convention. I have tried to provide balance as I highlighted the serious and the less serious aspects of his life. Many of the names used in this book are fictitious in order to protect the privacy of certain individuals.

Some of the information in the book I obtained by researching Baines's personal papers given to me by members of his family. Certain other facts or parts of

CHAPTER 1

Beach House

On Saturday night, December 8, 2007, I was at my beach pad at Hollywood Beach Mobile Home Park in Oxnard, California. I spent most weekends there during the school year and tried to make it my place of enjoyment when I was off from my teaching job for the summer or during the holidays. It was my haven away from the rigors of teaching P.E. and acting as Athletic Director at Granada Hills Charter High School. I and my wife, Debi, had another home in Simi Valley, California, where she was spending this same December weekend without me.

Watching TV had taken up most of my evening, along with preparing and consuming a dinner of barbecued steak, garlic cheese bread, and a green salad with blue cheese dressing, which is my favorite meal. Glasses of pinot noir complemented the meal and continued to ease me into the later hours of the evening.

Pressing the button on the television remote to find something to conclude my evening TV watching, I came upon a movie on AMC starring Gary Cooper. Since I am a big fan of the actor, I was curious. It had been on awhile, but after watching for a few minutes, I gathered that it was a movie about an ordinary man who had somehow gained nationwide celebrity status as an everyman's American hero—a guy named John Doe. Not knowing the name of the movie, and fascinated with the premise, I wanted to know the details I was missing.

So I decided to call my crazy, offbeat friend Baines Spivington, who was a genius when it came to TV and movie trivia and could answer any question I might have. It had been awhile since I'd talked to Baines, and I thought this would be an opportunity not only to get info about the movie, but also to get an update on how life had been treating him.

Baines filled me in on the plot of the movie, which was called *Meet John Doe*, and expressed life was treating him well. Seeing as both of us were tired, we agreed that we would continue our conversation on other meaningless topics the next morning.

After my movie ended, I watched the last part of *Thelma and Louise*, which Baines had been watching. When it ended, my eyelids were beginning to feel like lead; sleep was beckoning me. I rose from the love seat I was lying on, trudged down the hall to the master bedroom, and eased into bed.

I woke up the next morning and sipped coffee while I read the Sunday *Los Angeles Times* in bed. As was customary, I followed this leisurely activity with a shower and shave and then dressed and went to the local McDonald's for a late breakfast.

Over hotcakes, sausage, and another cup of coffee, I enjoyed listening to a group of old guys discussing a possible Democratic Party presidential candidate named Barack Obama. Their positive comments far outweighed their negative comments as they tried to determine whether, come election time, he might be their guy.

After McDonald's I paid a visit to Silver Strand Beach, where I watched surfers ripping waves on their boards offshore. At the same time, members of Alcoholics Anonymous were verbally ripping the evils of alcohol from their beach chairs onshore as they sucked down large mugs of coffee. After a fifteen-minute stay, I headed for home to plan out the rest of my day.

The light was blinking red on the kitchen phone when I arrived. Someone had tried to reach me while I was away. Probably Debi. It was too early for my brother, Bo, who lives in Hawaii. The kids were at church. I pushed the button on the phone to stop the blinking, put the phone to my ear, and listened to the anxious and worried voice of my wife.

"Rich, this is Debi! Call me, please!"

I dialed home, and Debi answered after the first ring. "Hello."

"Debi it's me. What's up?"

"Rich, sit down," Debi said in a worried tone on the other end of the line.

"What's happening, Debi? You sound upset."

"Are you seated?"

"I am. Yes. What's up?"

Debi explained calmly, "Baines Spivington is in the hospital. There was a fire in his condo last night, and he suffered burns and smoke inhalation. The police called me because Baines had our home phone number in his wallet. And when they searched him at the hospital looking for relatives to contact, we were it."

"You're kidding me, aren't you, Debi? This has got to be an effing joke. I talked to Baines last night."

"This is no joke. He may die, Rich. He's that serious according to the policeman. He's at the Grossman Burn Center on Van Nuys Boulevard in Sherman Oaks."

I suddenly felt anxious. *You need to be calm*, I thought. *Level-headed. Don't panic. You need to help your friend.*

Debi gave me directions to the hospital, a place I was familiar with, having visited it years ago when my mother received treatment for a severely burned hand that had required skin grafts and plastic surgery. Dr. Grossman had been her surgeon, and at the time he had been considered the best in the West, if not the world, in treating the most severe burn cases. Debi and I knew Baines was in the best place for his condition.

"I'm on my way to the hospital, Debi. First I need to contact Baines's brother, Monty, up north. Do you have Tim and Jane's phone number?"

"Who are they?"

"Baines's sister and his brother-in-law!"

"Why would we have their number?"

I felt frustrated because Debi had met them on several occasions. "Okay. I'll try the operator for information, Debi. See you at the hospital."

I hung up and dialed information.

"What city, please?" asked a polite male voice.

"Laguna Beach. Ah, maybe South Laguna Beach."

"Name and address, please."

"Ah, Tim. Tim Ball. I don't have an address."

Seconds dragged on like minutes. "There are two Tim Balls in Laguna Beach, sir."

"Give me both of them, please." I scribbled down the information on the magnetic notepad I'd pulled off the kitchen refrigerator door. "Thanks, man. You've been a big help."

I dialed the first Tim Ball. He was the wrong one, a professor at UC Irvine. My Tim Ball, Baines's brother-in-law, was a retired psychologist who had worked at Kaiser, in Laguna Hills, before his retirement. I dialed the second number and was greeted by an answering machine. I gave my name and my home and cell phone numbers and indicated that I needed to talk to Tim or Jane Ball. They knew me as one of Baines's best friends, having met me on numerous family occasions and out at restaurants. I hung up and hoped this might be the right Tim Ball and that he would receive my message.

I decided to call Monty knowing that if Tim tried to contact me, call waiting would pick up his call.

Monty's wife answered. "Hello."

"Trudy? This is Richard Hulse. Is Monty in?"

"Why, Rich, how are you?" she said in her usual polite voice. "Monty's not here. He's at our beach house at Sea Ranch." (I had called Trudy at the couple's home in Lafayette, near San Francisco.)

"Trudy, I need to get hold of him." I became light-headed and struggled to speak. I whispered slowly, "Trudy, Baines is in a burn hospital in Sherman Oaks. His condo caught fire, and he was trapped inside. I don't know all of the details. I just know I need to get hold of Monty."

I gained strength after taking in a slow deep breath. Nervous compassion came from the other end of the line.

"Oh my God, Rich," Trudy said softly. "Wait a minute." There was silence on Trudy's end for several seconds. When she returned, she continued, "Rich, it's Monty. He's on the other line. I told him briefly what you shared with me. He wants to know what's going with his brother. He is going to call you."

I gave her my phone number at the beach and then hung up to wait for Monty's call. In a short few seconds, my phone rang, and I pushed the answer button. The usually chipper Monty was anxious.

"Rich, wh-wh-what happened?"

"Your brother had a fire in his condominium. He's in the hospital, and he's in trouble, Monty." My lower eyelids began to well up with tears. I hesitated as I took in another slow deep breath. "I think you need to get down here, Monty, as soon as you can."

"I'm on my way."

"I'll pick you up at the airport. Just let me know which one and when."

"I'm going to drive down, Rich."

I was a bit taken by surprise. I emphasized in a strong tone, "From what little I know, your brother is in serious trouble! Don't you think you should fly?"

He repeated that he'd drive down. I wanted to end the conversation, because I was beginning to feel uncomfortable. Baines and Monty were not the closest of brothers. Sometimes years would go by without either one of them contacting the other. I bid Monty farewell and told him I would call as soon as I heard about any change in Baines's condition before he arrived in Los Angeles.

I tried Tim Ball once again and was greeted a second time by an answering machine. I hung up, frustrated.

I decided to call Baines's other best friend, Rowdy Ralphs, who lived in Studio City, not too far from the burn center in Sherman Oaks.

He answered in a subdued voice on the second ring. "Hello, Rowdy's residence."

"Rowdy, this is Richard Hulse!" I said anxiously.

Rowdy perked up on hearing my voice. "Daddy-o, what's up? Long time no see."

"I know, Rowdy." I paused. "Rowdy, Baines is in trouble."

I gave Rowdy the details I knew about what had happened to Baines and what I knew about his condition.

"Jesus Christ, Rich! I'm on my way to the hospital."

I told Rowdy that I was down at my beach pad and that he'd most likely get to the hospital before me. I told him about Monty. He didn't say anything, but I was sure he understood where Monty was coming from based on his knowledge of Monty's and Baines's relationship.

"Rich, I'll call you on my cell phone when I get to the hospital and let you know what's happening with Baines."

"Okay. Bye, Rowdy."

I dialed Harry La Force, a dear friend of mine and Baines who would give you the shirt off his back.

Harry answered his phone on the second ring in a friendly voice. "Hello, La Forces' residence."

"Harry, this is Richard."

"Daddy-o, rock 'n' roll, cool cat, jump and jive, man-a-live, psychedelic of the mind," Harry sang to me through the phone line—a regular greeting he had been accustomed to giving me over the years since the hippy sixties. Then, more calmly but still enthusiastically he asked, "What's up, Rich?"

I felt a tightening in my throat, and I again struggled to speak. "Harry, Baines Spivington is in the hospital in serious condition. His condo caught fire …" I paused, inhaled a deep breath, and continued. "His condo caught fire, and he suffered smoke inhalation and burns. He is at the Grossman Burn Center in Sherman Oaks on Van Nuys Boulevard."

"I know where it's located, Rich. I'm on my way. What about Rowdy Ralphs?"

I assured him that I had notified Rowdy and that he and Rowdy would precede me in arriving at the center, given that I was more than sixty miles away. I hung up and waited, hoping Tim Ball number two would call back and be the right one.

Ten minutes passed as I sat on the love seat in the family room, sipping from a mug of cold coffee. I decided to get on my way, hoping Tim or Jane would call me while I was in route to the hospital. I turned off the lights in my mobile home and shut down the heater. I exited through the back door, locked it, and was heading for my car when the phone inside my mobile home rang. Keys in hand, I sprinted back to the door, opened it, and ripped across the family room to answer the phone before it went silent.

"Hello."

"Hello, Rich?" This is Tim Ball. Long time no hear from you, Rich. What's happening? How's your family?"

I skipped the small talk and tried not to be blunt as I provided Tim with the reality of his brother-in-law Baines's situation and told him who I had contacted, including Monty. Being a psychologist, Tim calmly took in the information I had to share and assured me he and Jane were headed out right away to meet me, Rowdy, and Harry at the hospital. Tim figured it would be roughly an hour and fifteen minutes before he and Jane arrived the hospital.

I wished them a safe journey, and then we all got down to the business of heading to the hospital.

CHAPTER 2

Ballin' the Jack

I drove fast, ballin' the jack like a bat out of hell south on the Ventura Freeway. I knew it would take me at least an hour going seventy-five to get to Sherman Oaks. The freeway was clear, and I breezed along to my destination in my smooth-riding, late-model 2002 Toyota Camry with no highway patrol in sight.

I played music on the radio to assist me with my nerves, which were starting to fray. The Wave 94.7 radio station tried to soothe me through my car speakers with the sound of Kenny G's saxophone. Al Jarreau followed, then Lou Rawls, Al Green, Norah Jones, Boney James, and Barry White. Finally, Natalie Cole and her dead dad, Nat, ended my freeway journey with a father-daughter love song as I exited at Van Nuys Boulevard.

Left turn under the freeway. I headed north for one-quarter of a mile. I looked for a sign for the hospital, which I knew would be on my left. I saw the building but passed by it before I could turn in and find a parking spot.

I called Debi, who I knew would be at the hospital by now. She answered and directed me to a parking lot, where I saw my son-in-law, Jeremiah, and daughter, Catherine, waiting for me just outside the hospital entrance door. As I exited my vehicle, I was greeted with silence and warm, strong hugs from Jeremiah and Catherine.

We entered the hospital and wandered down a series of hallways before we met up with my wife and Harry La Force. Rowdy was there too, talking to an Asian—possibly Chinese—man who appeared to be a doctor. He and Rowdy looked serious as they spoke in silence a short distance away from the rest of us. I gave Debi a big hug and exchanged hugs with my friend Harry, too.

I thought about what had transpired in a few short hours. I had talked to Baines at about 10:30 p.m. the night before. We were supposed to continue our conversation at 11:00 a.m. this morning. And here I was at 1:30 p.m. wondering whether I would ever talk to my friend again.

Rowdy broke from his conversation, and the doctor left the hallway through a door. Rowdy approached us with bad news. He confirmed that the man he'd been talking to was one of the doctors handling Baines's case. Rowdy shared that Baines had suffered burns on his arms as paramedics removed him from the back bedroom of his condo and raced to get him to safety. Worse, Baines had inhaled a great amount of smoke, and his lungs had suffered a great deal of damage; he could barely breathe. His heart was barely beating even with the help of the cardio machine the hospital staff had attached to our friend. The scene seemed surreal to me.

Harry asked Rowdy if he could see Baines, and Rowdy confirmed the doctor said each of us could visit him one at a time. Harry walked through the same door the doctor had used to exit the hallway. Rowdy continued to fill us in on what he had learned from the paramedics. They told him when they arrived on the scene both the front door and patio door to Baines's third-story condo were open. They said a neighbor mentioned to the firemen that he had seen a cat exiting the flaming, smoke-filled condominium through the open patio door. This seemed odd to all of us, because Baines did not have a cat.

Harry returned from Baines's hospital room and reiterated what Rowdy had shared with us about Baines's condition. He confirmed that Baines's arms didn't look to be the problem. He told us Baines was hardly breathing, and the doctors had told Harry that Baines's heart was giving out.

We tried to make sense of this information as we tried to piece together what had happened to Baines and his condominium. Rowdy added that according to the firemen, the fire had originated in Baines's condominium and spread to his next-door neighbor's condominium.

I knew that I could see Baines, but I chose not to. I shuddered as I contemplated that the end of his life was near. Even when a person has passed on and I attend a funeral, I avoid looking in the open casket. The only dead person I had ever viewed was my father as he lay propped up in his hospital bed in the intensive care unit at St. Joseph Hospital in Burbank, California. Baines was not dead yet, but I chose to picture him at his happiest, sitting in his beach chair at Hollywood Beach, eyeballing bikini-clad girls and sucking down a can of ice-cold Coors Light beer.

I thought about the conversation I'd had with Baines the night before. I tried to recall if he'd said anything that perhaps would have indicated he was distraught; anything that might have caused him to end up at the Grossman Burn Center.

"Spivington's residence."

"Baines!"

"Rick!"

"How's it going, man? I've been meaning to call you as we haven't talked much lately."

"Me too, Daddy. What's up?"

"I am down at the beach, and I am watching a film on AMC. It's a movie with Gary Cooper and Barbara Stanwyck. Cooper's character is called John Doe, at least in some of the parts of the movie. He's referred to as Long John Willoughby, too."

"I'm into Thelma and Louise myself. The film you're watching is a great film, Daddy! It's called Meet John Doe. It's a Frank Capra classic. Not his best-known picture, but one of them. A Capraesque bit of genius! Pure genius! I've seen it several times. It was one of Ethan's favorite films. I bought him a copy that he watched over and over and over."

"I think I remember your dad talking to me about it some time ago just before he passed away. I'm turning down the volume so I can hear you better. Go on."

"The story is about a newspaper columnist, Stanwyck, who has been laid off from her job at The New Bulletin. Her pissed-off character, Ann Mitchell, prints a fake letter in the newspaper that causes social upheaval, the letter being a suicide note from a John Doe who is protesting society's ills."

"Sounds a tad bizarre."

"There's more. Mitchell finds a real guy to portray Doe, a former baseball player named John Willoughby, who becomes a hero across the United States for his political philosophy, thinks he is being taken advantage of, and contemplates suicide."

"I think I am at that part right now, Baines."

"Anyway, Daddy, the guy is going to make reference to Jesus as a historical John Doe who has already died for the sake of humanity. You need to watch it again to get the total picture. I am going back to Thelma and Louise. It's one of my all-time favorite flicks."

"Jesus stuff? Genius! Fine, Baines. Thanks for the info. Thelma and Louise, huh? I'll probably watch it after the Doe movie is over. I'll call you tomorrow morning. I have some stuff to share with you, and I need your opinion on a few things."

"I'll be waiting for your call tomorrow. After 11:00 a.m., please, Daddy. Ta-ta."

"Ta. Tomorrow, Baines. After 11:00."

I couldn't think of anything terribly unusual about the previous night's conversation that might cause Baines to do something dangerous or stupid and risk his life. We had agreed to talk again the next morning. I wondered, was this the last conversation I would have with my dear friend of forty-two years?

Time passed slowly as we all waited for Jane and Tim to arrive from Laguna Beach. Baines's life was "going" fast according to the doctor who had talked to Rowdy and Harry. I paced the hallway. Jeremiah and Catherine purchased sandwiches from the cafeteria. We used the restroom. Conversation reverted to talk about our families as everyone shared what had been going on since we last saw one another.

The doctor reentered the hall and told us that Baines's was close to death, and the only thing keeping him alive was the life support system. I told the doctor that Baines's sister and brother-in-law were driving up from Laguna Beach and were expected to arrive anytime.

As the doctor returned to attend to Baines, a car entered the parking lot in front of the hospital. It was Jane and Tim. They tried to be pleasant as they entered the hospital and greeted us. Rowdy told them what he knew. They realized they had to decide whether Baines was to remain on life support, and they asked to see the doctor.

Within minutes after their arrival, Baines was taken off life support and he passed away. All of us were stunned as we all in our own ways tried to console and comfort one another. Jane and Tim assured us they would stay in town for the night and make plans to assure Baines was properly taken care of. We all offered to assist Jane and Tim and the Spivington family in whatever way we could. Catherine and Jeremiah said a prayer for Baines. Jane and Tim thanked us. Tim indicated that Monty would arrive the next day and assist Tim and Jane with the plans for Baines.

CHAPTER 3

On the Road Again

The drive home for me was agony. Besides the fact that Baines was dead, I dreaded the job I offered to do for Jane and Tim—call Baines's other friends to let them know he had tragically passed away. I pulled up onto my driveway, and my cell phone rang. It was Monty. He explained he planned to join Jane and Tim after he drove down from Lafayette. He asked me questions about Baines, and I answered the best I could. I was mentally exhausted, and I repeated the information shared by Rowdy and Harry, including what the Chinese doctor told them, and the decision Jane had needed to make regarding prolonging Baines's suffering or letting his passing allow him final peace.

Monty told me he was grateful for all of our help and said he would contact me soon with the details he, Tim, and Jane worked out regarding what they would do with Baines's body. He mentioned there would be an autopsy. There would be police and fire reports to determine the cause of the fire. And, there was Baines's stuff, if anything survived. What to do with it? He touched on the topics of whether Baines had a will? Insurance? Debts? His three cars? His girlfriend?

In my house, over some Smirnoff on the rocks, I began my task of calling Baines's friends to let them know of his tragic death.

I called Norm Johnson first—an old friend Baines had not seen for years. I told him what I knew, and his response scared me.

"What in the hell happened, Huulis? Was he murdered? Suicide?" (Huulis is a nickname Norm coined for me many years before based on an experience I had in the Navy Reserve.)

"I don't know, Norm. I haven't had time to think about those things. I'm just telling you our buddy is dead."

"Stock Norm," Baines would have responded, knowing Norm cares about and thinks about many things to the extreme.

I called Mike Sweet, Jerry O'Gill, and also called Ron and Linda Merriman. All were old friends of Baines. They responded with shock—disbelief. My task became tedious as I tried to call as many of Baines's friends as I could. I didn't call them all, because I did not have contact information for all of them. Some of the friends Baines hadn't seen for years—Rudy Ripulski; Stein Stevens; Dom Taws; Dennis Dobber; Christine Stillwater—all friends from the past who cared a great deal for Baines and Baines for them. The problem—how to get hold of them. It would be months before I contacted them with the exception of Christine Stillwater. I discovered on a social network website on my computer that she passed away in 2001. There was no cause of death.

CHAPTER 4

Tim Ball Calls

On Monday I received a call on my cell phone from Tim Ball. I was at school, but I had time to talk, because it was my conference period. He assured me that he, Jane, and Monty were on top of dealing with Baines's affairs. He told me he had contacted Baines's girlfriend, Fleur. He indicated that she was quite upset with the news of Baines's passing. I didn't tell Tim my thoughts about Baines's girlfriend or her reaction. I didn't like the woman or the way she treated Baines during the years she was his girlfriend.

Tim continued our conversation by inviting me to meet with him, Monty, and Rowdy Ralphs at Baines's condominium on Saturday. He said we would go through the condo and salvage what we could. He assured me there may be mementos of Baines's that Rowdy and I might wish to take and keep. He indicated that the autopsy on Baines's body would be done by then, hopefully revealing what took the life from my friend. He said Baines's cremation would be planned, but he provided me no details because he had none. I struggled to get through the week, anticipating that Saturday was going to be a sad and difficult day.

The four of us arrived at Baines's condominium long before he would have been awake. It was just shy of 10:00 a.m. The front of the condominium complex showed evidence of the fire. There was rubble on the lawn near the front-stairs entrance to the lobby—burned overstuffed chairs; a melted TV; a charred metal TV stand; burned dining room chair frames; and a burned dining room table. The smell of smoke lingered outside the building. It became progressively stronger as we entered the lobby and took the elevator to the third floor, where Baines's condo was located. The walls in the hallway were scarred with smoke. The hallway carpet reeked from the combination of burning building and the fire hose water used to douse the flames the weekend before. The damage to the condominium next door was hidden behind a plastic sheet hung across a door-less entrance.

The four of us entered Baines's condominium. There was no light save for that which crept into the hallways from the empty holes of what once had been aluminum-framed glass windows. Some rooms were brighter because of the angle of the morning light. There was no furniture in the living room or the dining room. The kitchen had none, but a refrigerator remained with its white exterior paint bubbled black from the heat of the fire.

The walls and ceilings of both bedrooms were covered with smoke but had not caught fire. The bed in Baines's bedroom was gone. It had more than likely been removed to prevent it from catching fire. A small wooden desk remained in the bedroom along with a metal filing cabinet.

The other bedroom had bookshelves housing books and tapes of music, and there was a desk with a laptop computer resting on top of it. There were various items wrapped in paper inside a closet. Some items were on the floor and some items rested on the closet shelves.

We started in Baines's bedroom, which was well-lit. Tim Ball suggested we look for valuables first such as credit cards, car keys, bank and checking account information, a cell phone, insurance papers, and a will. We didn't have any luck in finding any of these items in plain sight. We determined that none of us had heard Baines indicate he had a will.

We looked in Baines's closet. The clothing and his shoes in the closet were not burned, but smoke damaged. Rowdy and I looked at one another as we discovered Baines's collection of porn movies stacked neatly on top of one another against the wall in the closet, opposite his clothes and shoes. I estimate there were probably fifty movies in his two-stack collection. We said nothing to Tim or Monty, but we winked at one another, indicating that we knew that Baines's nights at home alone were not without some sexual excitement.

Rowdy tried to open the filing cabinet that had stood next to Baines's missing bed. It was locked shut. I found some small keys in the top drawer of Baines's bedroom desk. Rowdy tried each key in the cabinet's one lone lock. No luck. We decided that busting open the lock was the solution to getting to the cabinet's contents. Rowdy was very good with all things mechanical, and he attacked the cabinet lock with a hammer and a flathead screwdriver Tim had provided.

Rowdy made short work of the lock with four hefty swings of the hammer. Inside the cabinet were manila folders. Tim took them out and examined the contents of each folder. He did not share the exact contents with Rowdy, Monty, or me, but he said he believed these were Baines's important papers.

Tim asked me to see what was in the desk. It had three drawers on the right side, all of them the same size. There were photographs in the first one. One was of my daughter Catherine when she was little girl. There were other photographs of family members and friends that Baines had accumulated over the years. None were in an album. There were also business-size envelopes, pens and pencils, erasers, paper clips, a small bottle of white LePage's craft glue, and a small handheld stapler. This was Baines's mini-storage of stationery supplies.

I closed the first drawer and opened the second drawer. Inside I found a topless shoe box filled with tickets, all sorts of tickets of different sizes, prices, venues, and events. Some were torn in half. Some were whole. Some were new. Some were old. These, I knew, represented tickets to Baines's life. I recognized many of the events and activities. I had attended many of them with Baines. But unlike him, I had thrown most of my tickets away.

Coliseum Relays; USC football; a few Rose Bowls; Raiders; Rams; Dorothy Chandler Pavilion; USC basketball; UCLA Bruins basketball during the John Wooden years; the Ahmanson Theater; drive-in and walk-in movie theaters; Lakers basketball; Yosemite; high school championship games; all sorts of high school games.

I thought, *Tickets! Tickets! Tickets! Baines's life hadn't been boring, at least a lot of the time.*

I showed them to Tim and Rowdy and asked Tim what I should do with them. He said he did not want them. I offered them to Monty. He told me to keep them. I offered them to Rowdy and received the same response. (It would not be until two years later after I retired from teaching that I would reexamine the tickets.)

I opened the third drawer. Inside there were three manila envelope folders stuffed with papers. I handed them to Tim one at a time. He thumbed through each folder and briefly shared their contents.

One folder contained short stories and other assignments Baines had submitted to his English teachers at California State University, Northridge along with stories apparently written by other students. The name Wally Graves came to my mind when Tim told me what the first folder contained. Wally had been one of Baines's few teaching heroes while attending CSUN. I remembered that Baines had been Wally's teaching assistant for several semesters during his pursuit of a Bachelor of Arts Degree in English, and under Graves, Baines taught several first and second-year English classes.

The second folder contained two polished final copies of Baines's master's thesis, *An Analytical Comparison of the Writings of Emile Zola and Frank Norris*. Completing the folder's contents were several drafts of the thesis with diacritical markings, comments, and suggestions from his master's thesis sponsor, Dr. Richard Abcarian. I had seen Baines work his ass off for three years in his pursuit of a Master's Degree in English. By finishing this thesis, which compared the naturalist writings of these two well-known authors, he not only succeeded in earning his Master's Degree, he also succeeded in conquering the self-imposed fear that he wasn't a critical thinker and writer.

Tim thought the third folder contained Baines's personal writings. He glanced at them briefly and then handed the three folders back to me. "These are yours, Rich, if you want them."

I offered them to Monty, but he declined. Rowdy declined my offer, as well. I set the folders aside, not realizing until later examination that they contained stories about how Baines had perceived his life.

We entered the other bedroom. The laptop computer appeared dead even though it was plugged into an electrical socket. Rowdy tried to make it work with no success. Music tapes in plastic containers might have been salvageable, but none of us were interested in them. The wrapped items in the closet were pieces of silver. There were several ornamented pitchers and several platters; one with the name Spivington inscribed on its smoke-covered surface. There were various spoons, knives, and ladles, too. Tim thought most of the items belonged to Ethan and Isabel. Some he remembered belonging to Isabel and her first husband, Leonard, my newly deceased friend's father.

Monty indicated he wanted none of the items. Tim tried to give me and Rowdy more pieces than each of us wanted. I struggled to be polite, and I gave in to Tim. Rowdy did, too. The short period of time we had been in Baines's condominium has taken its toll on us. I could see it on Tim's and Rowdy's face. I felt like shit as I pondered the reality that Baines Spivington was dead.

That evening over half of a six-pack of Coors, I reflected on the metamorphosis of Baines and his world over the forty-plus years I had known him.

When I first met him, he carried 175 pounds on his six-foot-two frame. Over the years, his love for rich food and heavy intake of liquor gradually increased his weight to more than 200 hundred pounds. He was never skinny but never became what one would describe as fat. In fact, his lower body was always well toned. He had athletic muscular thighs and calves that developed as he played basketball in high school, college, and recreationally, thereafter.

When his playing days were over, Baines took vigorous late afternoon walks around his Dickens Avenue neighborhood, which allowed him to maintain the strength of his lower body. On many an occasion I joined Baines in this activity. Along with this physical exercise, Baines exercised his mind as he checked out the many young neighborhood ladies who jogged by him. Every once in a while, one would blush as she saw Baines's eyes cherish her well-developed athletic body.

A young mustached Baines with long blond hair gave way in later years to a clean-shaven Baines with much shorter salon-sculpted white hair. He had a long slender face with a long slender nose. On the bridge of his nose he wore glasses for reading, seeing distance, or shading his eyes from the sun. Baines had a careful way of smiling, making sure not to fully express his emotions when something funny occurred that he did not fully understand. Baines was a shy person, especially when put in public places and large gatherings. He admitted to me many times that his shyness caused him to struggle to have fun.

As an adult, Baines worked most of his life for Ralphs Grocery Company as a clerk and cashier. He attended Valley College, where he earned an Associate's Degree in Physical Education and Theater Arts. He continued his studies at Cal State University, Northridge, where he earned a Bachelor of Arts in Physical Education. When he was rejected as a student teacher candidate by the Physical Education Department at CSUN because the faculty questioned whether he was "healthy" (Baines had a pale complexion), instead of directing his energy to convince the adamant department to reverse its decision, he decided to direct his energy toward the pursuit of a Bachelor of Arts Degree in English.

After receiving his BA in English at CSUN, Baines decided he wanted to become an elementary school teacher. He transferred to California State University, Los Angeles which is known for its excellent elementary teaching credential program. Halfway through the completion of his credential classes, Baines decided teaching elementary school was not for him. He was not willing to give up a lifestyle he enjoyed—one that included staying up until the early hours of the morning watching TV and consuming Bombay Gin and Smirnoff Vodka. Baines was a night owl. Waking at 11:00 a.m. was early for him.

Next in line for Baines was the pursuit of a Master's Degree in English. He returned to CSUN, and after three years under the guidance of English Professor Richard Abcarian, Baines was awarded his Master's Degree in English.

Eventually Baines would take care of his parents full-time until his mother, Isabel, passed away and a few years later Baines's stepfather, Ethan B. Schwartz, passed away.

Much of what I reflected on that evening, I knew would not be included in Baines's obituary. As far as I know, one was never published.

CHAPTER 5

Saturday at the Office

Almost two weeks had passed since Baines died. It was Saturday morning, and I was home, not at the beach. I decided to go to school and complete some athletics paperwork. I climbed into my car and motored on several local surface streets. I took the Ronald Reagan Freeway east, exited at Reseda Boulevard, and made my way to Zelzah Avenue, where I passed through the gate and onto the boys' P.E. blacktop. I sat in my car contemplating what I had to do in the boys' P.E. office. A ridiculous idea interrupted my thoughts about work— *Why not call Baines's cell phone and see if it is still active? His cell phone was not found in his condo. What are the chances it still has a charge and its voicemail will answer my call?*

I dialed his number, and his phone rang. I anticipated Baines's recorded greeting, "At the sound of the beep, please leave your name and number," followed by a pause and then an emphatic, "Thank you." But at ring three, instead of hearing Baines's greeting, I heard a Spanish-speaking male voice. I was shocked. I didn't understand what the voice on the other end of the line was saying. Suddenly I had the chills, and I hung up without saying anything to the Spanish speaker.

Who in the fuck was that? I asked myself as I sat there dumbfounded. Disbelief struck me hard. *Who had Baines's cell phone? How did he get it? Where was this guy?*

I had Tim Ball's number in my cell phone contacts, and I called it. His answering machine picked up and recorded my message telling him what happened after I dialed Baines's cell phone number. He called me back about a half hour later as I sat at my desk processing athletics paperwork. His response was like mine— disbelief. He told me Jane had a lady friend who spoke Spanish and might be able to help us find out who had Baines's phone and why. Tim explained it might take some time to reach her, because she was a busy woman who worked for the U.S. Department of Homeland Security.

After Tim hung up, I thought, perhaps I had dialed a wrong number, not Baines's cell phone number. I checked the menu of outgoing calls on my cell phone, and the menu clearly showed I called the correct number. I tried to get back to work, but I only fidgeted through the papers on my desk. I was anxious to know who had Baines's cell phone. I decided to leave school, knowing that I had very little interest in my work. I drove home and spent all evening waiting for Tim to call me. He didn't call that evening, and I decided not to call him.

CHAPTER 6

Baines's Cell Phone

Two days passed before Tim Ball got back to me regarding the stranger who'd answered Baines's cell phone. When he did call, I was teaching volleyball skills to my second-period ninth-grade coed P.E. class. In circular groups of five to six, my students were in the process of bumping and passing a volleyball demanding little attention from me as they proceeded through the drill. I was able to talk to Tim on my cell phone without any interruption. Having anxiously waited for two days, I was doubly anxious to hear Tim's findings.

"Good morning, Tim. What's up?"

"Good morning, Rich. Sorry for the delay in getting back to you. It took me a while to get hold of Jane's friend, and it took her some time to try to make contact with whoever possesses Baines's cell phone."

"What's the story, Tim? I hope there's some sense to this weird happening. To me it's got to be some sort of bullshit." (I was not within earshot of my students.)

Without verbally reacting to my expletive, Tim continued. "Rich, Jane's friend said she dialed Baines's cell phone and a lady speaking Spanish answered the phone, not a man. Jane's friend explained to the lady that the phone she was using was Baines Spivington's phone and that he had died in a fire in his condominium. When she asked the lady how she had acquired the phone, the woman responded that Baines had given it to her husband."

"That's hard for me to believe, Tim. I know Baines, and he would never do something like that. He was very possessive with his things like his cell phone. Perhaps he was a workman at the condo after the fire and found it?"

"Don't know, Rich. Don't know. Jane's friend didn't go there. She only shared with me what I have told you. Anyway, I have canceled Baines's cell phone service, and they said they won't charge for the service as of the day Baines died."

"Gotcha, Tim."

I paused, wondering if there was anything more for me to ask or say that made sense. I thought to ask whether the police had been contacted regarding the phone, but dismissed this idea. After all, Tim was a smart man. Baines's sister was smart. They had probably thought of the idea. Baines was their relative, not mine. What business was it of mine? I was dismayed and tired. My friend of forty-two years was gone.

I wrapped up my phone conversation with Tim. "Thanks for your efforts, Tim. I have to get back to my class. My best to Jane. Catch you later, man."

"Take care, Rich. I'll talk to you later in the week regarding arrangements for Baines."

Later in the week I received a mild shock. Tim called me and told me the family had put Baines's ashes to rest at sea. I was nearly speechless as I pondered what

Tim shared. I thought, *How dare they put my buddy's ashes in the Pacific Ocean without including me and my family and Baines's other friends?* I tried to remain calm and did not question what Baines's family had done with his remains. Tim also shared that an autopsy had been performed on Baines, but the results of the cause of death were still pending.

Maintaining my composure, I thanked Tim for letting me know what they had done with Baines's ashes. I thought putting his ashes in the salt water of the Pacific Ocean seemed appropriate for the *pacific* Baines I'd known. I mentioned to Tim that I thought perhaps someone should arrange some sort of memorial or wake for Baines. Tim agreed but thought it best to wait awhile before anything could be arranged.

CHAPTER 7

Little Tony's

When I told my wife, Debi, Baines's ashes were now part of the Pacific Ocean, she thought I was making a sick joke. She knew how close I was to Baines, and she knew to exclude me from the ceremony at sea bordered on ridiculous. Over the years she knew I was more of a brother to Baines than his own brother, Monty. She said the whole thing did not seem right to her. Not intending to make a pun, she said, "The whole thing seemed fishy."

When I mentioned to her I had talked to Tim about someone arranging some type of gathering to remember and honor Baines, she did not hesitate to support the idea that I should organize it and put on such a gathering. She said it would be therapeutic for me and give me some closure on the fact that my longtime buddy indeed was now in a place of peace. Debi suggested that by me making the contacts of those who might wish to attend such a gathering, it would spare Baines's family the task of contacting them. As well, she pointed out that the family knew only a few of those who might wish to attend anyway, and I agreed.

When I told Debi that I knew the perfect place to hold the memorial, we shouted in unison, "Little Tony's!"

Some of the better times that my friends and I had spent with Baines Spivington had taken place at Little Tony's Pizzeria in North Hollywood. I drank my first beer in public there at the age of eighteen. Baines, who was twenty-one, bought it for me. In fact, he bought beer there for all of his underage co-workers from the North Hollywood Ralphs Supermarket, which was conveniently located across Lankershim Boulevard from the pizzeria.

It was at Little Tony's I broke up with my then girlfriend and future wife, Debi, over pizza and beer. It was at Little Tony's Ralphs workers celebrated the life of Doc "Miracle Miles" Kerrigan. He died at ninety years of age and had been a regular at the supermarket who the management allowed to rummage through the trash bins on the dock behind the market. He was the local lovable neighborhood character who no one could find fault with, and he always brought a smile to your face. Doc also served as the younger workers' eccentric adopted grandfather figure, giving them words of wisdom and advice on how they could prolong their lives with a daily consumption of carrageen moss.

When Debi and I got back together and decided marriage was in order, at the age of twenty-four I had my bachelor party at Little Tony's. Baines Spivington led the charge ordering pitcher after pitcher of cold Coors draft.

Many times over the years, Baines and I, and our buddies and their girlfriends engaged in good and sad times at Little Tony's. Thus, Little Tony's would hopefully serve as the proper venue to honor Baines.

When I contacted Tim Ball and Monty Spivington, neither had an objection to my idea and choice of venue. I told them I would research Little Tony's policies for big parties and see if they had enough room to hold our group. I told them I would contact Baines's friends and let them know the arrangements, such as day and time. They encouraged me to proceed with their blessings and thanks. I was now off and running on my buddy Baines's behalf. I knew in my heart that Baines would not have chosen anywhere but Little Tony's for his friends and relatives to celebrate his life.

I arranged to have Baines's celebration on a Saturday. This seemed convenient for all of his friends I contacted who said they would attend. (It would be months after the celebration of Baines's life that I would finally contact some of his older friends he had known in high school.) Little Tony's had a banquet room to serve our needs. This room had been added on to a rebuilt Little Tony's that had burned down years before. Pizza, beer, and wine were the exclusive choices for those who attended. The pizza remained the same greasy delight that many of us had enjoyed back in our working days at Ralphs Lankershim.

I was the host of this Little Tony's event, and I asked my daughter Catherine to initiate the celebration of Baines's life with a prayer. Emotional, reverent testimonials for Baines followed.

Norm Johnson started with his love of the writing experiences he'd had with Baines in their twenties when they penned criticism of the Vietnam War with their play, *Plastic Bag*. Norm explained the play was a story of the savageness of this conflict and the arrival home of mangled dead boys encased in body bags. He explained that the pair's consumption of copious amounts of red wine had served to inspire the ink they put to paper.

Jerry O'Gill shared the Hawaii trip he, Baines, Norm, and I had experienced in 1968. He recalled how Baines, the driver of our rental car on Kauai, had maneuvered through a jungle pathway to a pristine white sand beach being gently kissed by small, clear-blue waves at sunset. He revisited the evening cocktail parties we attended at Coco Palms Hotel that allowed us to get freely intoxicated at the expense of the owner, Grace Buscher.

Rowdy Ralphs partially credited Baines for what he had become—a microbiology lecturer at UCLA. Without Baines's encouragement he said, he might have continued with a career as a cashier at Ralphs Sherman Oaks grocery store. He also credited Baines for being a major force by supporting him in his quest to earn a Master's Degree in Science and then a Doctorate in Science.

Izzy Michaelson highlighted the cross-country road trip by car he once took with Baines and Harry La Force in route to Pittsburgh, which was the La Force clan's hometown. He spoke of visiting Notre Dame University in South Bend, Indiana; Boston; the Grand Canyon; Canada. He shared that on their trip, they enjoyed drinking lots of beer, throwing a football around at rest stops, photographing pretty girls, and taking snap shots of unusual or funny billboards or street signs. He finished by telling us he had a silent video of their experience and would make copies on a compact disc for anyone who wished to have one.

As everyone took their turn, it was evident that Baines had touched and enriched these people's lives.

I was the last to speak on Baines's behalf. I described the great parties Baines had thrown in his early twenties—the Spivy Bashes. (Spivy was a nickname coined by Baines's buddies, who otherwise called him Spivington.) I talked about our travels together over the years. The many sporting events he and I attended. Finally, I shared that not long after Baines died, I had assigned him to help my father with his job in heaven— the creating of beautiful sunsets. One recent cloudy evening, I told those gathered, I was sitting in my beach chair at the Hollywood Beach shore when a couple passed me and commented that it was too bad there was not a sunset. As I agreed with them, I thought of Baines and my dad and their jobs as creators of sunsets. Suddenly, as the couple left me behind, the cloudy sky above the Channel Islands exploded into a sea of red. This glowing hue appeared for several seconds and then faded into the gray that had preceded it. I felt sure that Baines and my dad had given me a sign that they knew their jobs in heaven.

When the celebration for Baines came to an end, Tim Ball paid for the food and booze with a plastic credit card—the method Baines always used to pay for anything and everything.

CHAPTER 8

After Little Tony's

Not long after Baines's Little Tony's gathering, I managed to contact two of his high school buddies whom he had not seen or talked to in years. I contacted Stein Stevens online through Classmates.com. I had signed up for this online service to see what my fellow North Hollywood classmates were about, and I saw his name appear on the roster of North Hollywood graduates. I e-mailed him, asking if he was the Stein Stevens who had been a friend of Baines Spivington. He responded he was, asked me how Baines was doing, and said to tell him hello. I made phone contact with Stein and told him the sad news of Baines's passing. Needless to say, he was shocked and sad. Besides Baines being his friend, he said Baines also had been his chauffeur whenever he needed a ride somewhere, Baines being the only one of his friends in high school who had a car.

The second friend I contacted by phone was Dom Taws, who lived in Thousand Oaks. I found him in the telephone book. During our phone conversation, he also expressed his shock and sorrow at Baines's passing and echoed what Stein Stevens had said about Baines being his chauffeur during high school, too. Both confirmed Baines's response each time one of them or both had sought a ride—"I need a quarter for gas." I had met Stevens and Taws once in the distant past, but I couldn't (and still can't) recall when or where. They both agreed that someday we should all meet and reminisce about Baines and fill in the years we shared or missed with him. This meeting hasn't come to fruition yet, but may in the future.

I tried to contact a mutual friend of Baines's and mine, Rudy Ripulski, who lives in Colorado. Although Baines and I had both lost contact with him, I knew that Rudy would want to know Baines's fate and what Baines had done during the lost years of their friendship. Baines and I had been in his wedding years before in Ventura, California. Two days after he and Judy exchanged their wedding vows, he swept her away to live with him in the Rocky Mountain state.

I finally made contact with him after visiting my son, daughter-in-law, and grandkids who live in Centennial, Colorado. I had gone there to visit them, and while there, I had tried everything I could to find Rudy and failed. Upon returning to California, I was persistent and determined to find Rudy.

Finally, one Sunday afternoon, I made contact. I had gone to my beach house to spend the weekend and was using the Internet. I knew that Rudy had probably retired and that an attempt to find him employed somewhere might prove futile. But I thought perhaps one of his boys might be employed somewhere in the state of Colorado. I typed in the name Ripulski and the word business. To my surprise a business owned by a David Ripulski appeared on the screen. I peered at it with particular interest, because besides colorful graphics, there was a photograph of someone who looked like Rudy.

I called the posted business number and received a recorded message from the owner of the company, a David Ripulski. At the sound of the beep I asked David whether his dad was Rudy Ripulski and told him who I was. I hung up, and no more than three minutes later, my cell phone started ringing, showing a Colorado number. I answered hello to be greeted by the voice of Rudy Ripulski. Finally, contact had been made.

I told Rudy what had happened to Baines and tried to answer the few questions he had about him. Since they had not spoken for years, I gave him a summary profile of Baines's life since they had last seen one another. We agreed that we would talk on the phone from time to time. I told him that my son, daughter-in-law, and grandchildren lived in Colorado and that the opportunity to get together with him and Judy was a matter of when Debi and I would fly back to the Rocky Mountain state.

It was after the conversations with Stein, Dom, and Rudy that I decided I wanted to write about our dead friend. I had thought about it many times before as a way I could possibly lessen my pain. And after all, there was no obituary for Baines that I knew of. There was no headstone or plaque with an epitaph for Baines. He deserved something other than the postmortem recognition he had received at Little Tony's. Perhaps family and friends might want to read what I would write about Baines. *Who knows?* I thought. *Maybe someday I might even try to publish Baines's story in book form for other people to read.* Debi agreed that writing about him was an excellent decision, and she offered me encouragement. So I began to engage in the writing process that would conclude as a memorial to my crazy friend, Baines Spivington.

What would I write about? As I pondered this question, I started putting together an outline. I wanted to highlight his life. It had to include Baines's personality traits; his happiness; his depression; his adventures and misadventures; his friends and family; his education, and his basic lifestyle. I wanted to include what he had taught me; what I had taught him; and what we had learned together. It took me awhile to start writing, but once I did, the words flowed. I also had several of the stories Baines had written as assignments for his college English classes to refer to. One in particular showed me a Baines that many people did not know.

CHAPTER 9

Monty First

Long before I knew Baines Spivington, I knew his brother, Monty, whom I met in 1959 while in seventh grade at Walter Reed Junior High School. Monty and I had gardening class together with Mr. Danforth. Initially we did not seem to have anything in common, until one day during class, a tall skinny American Indian classmate named Ron Whitesleeves started stomping our neatly planted rows of radishes and carrots, which we were growing in plots next to one another. Shocked, angered, and dismayed at what was happening, Monty and I were suddenly thrown together in a relationship stemming from the destruction of our carefully sown vegetable garden by this class terrorist. We quickly finked on Whitesleeves as he continued to stomp other students' plots beyond ours. When the dust had cleared and our plots lay ruined, he was severally disciplined for his actions, with Danforth and the school administration suspending him. He was not to return to school until his parents conferenced with Mr. Danforth and the school's vice principal, Mr. Fryers.

That was the last time Ron hit our veggies and the last time he participated in the gardening class. They transferred him to electric shop, and we never did learn what had caused him to go off on his fellow classmates' plots.

After this incident, Monty and I felt a common bond. We were both victims, being our plots were destroyed by the feet of this other student.

It was not long after this incident that we became closer geographically, too, when my family moved into Monty's neighborhood. Our house was less than a mile from La Casa de la Puerta Roja—the name engraved on the red wooden front gate of the Schwartz/Spivington family residence. Besides being in the same gardening class, and living close to one another, we often crossed paths when walking to and from school and when riding bicycles around the neighborhood. Occasionally we attended the same Sunday school classes at the First Christian Church of North Hollywood. We continued to have classes together throughout junior high school, and when we graduated and entered North Hollywood High School, the pattern continued.

It was in high school I began hearing about Monty's brother, Baines, in bits and pieces. The way Monty talked about him, he seemed like an icon. Or, at least a neighborhood idol or hero. He had graduated the year before we entered high school, and he was one of the few in his age group to have a car—a maroon '57 Chevy—the popular model with the small tail fins on the rear of the car. Baines had a girlfriend, Cathy, who was one of the most beautiful women in the San Fernando Valley.

Baines worked at Ralphs Supermarket as a clerk/cashier and had plenty of spending money to use for dinners out, movies, and sporting events, which he could not get enough of. That standard request Baines made of his friends when they needed a ride—"I need a quarter for gas"—allowed Baines to attend many social events, including sporting events, without putting a strain on his wallet. He and his buddies and their girlfriends went everywhere. Cathy was the youngest in the crowd but joined in nicely with these postgraduate party animals.

CHAPTER 10

Getting To Know You

It was not until September 1965 that I began to know Baines as both a co-worker and a friend. In June of that year, I graduated from high school, and the next two and a half months of that summer, I spent working in Hawaii as a busboy at the Coco Palms Hotel on the Garden Island of Kauai. This had been arranged by my father, Jerry Hulse, who was the travel editor at the *Los Angeles Times*; this was his way of rewarding me for graduating from high school and allowing me the opportunity to *grow up*. Upon returning from a wonderful working summer, I was looking forward to attending San Fernando Valley State College in the fall. Needing spending money, I applied for a job as a box boy at the Lankershim Ralphs Supermarket in North Hollywood where Baines worked.

The first day of school arrived, and I was offered a job at Ralphs that same day. When I arrived home in the afternoon, my mother told me the store manager, a Harold Chanaga, had called while I was attending morning classes. Although I was excited about the job offer, I considered the timing a bit off, since I had just started college that day and was already frustrated from the reading load that had been bestowed on me by my professors. But I didn't expect that I would start work that day, so I went to the store to accept the job and meet my new boss.

When I arrived in the store's parking lot and parked my car, I was surprised to see an old friend nearby. Ricky, who lived in my old neighborhood, was wearing a Ralphs' apron and gathering the shopping carts customers had left behind. I got out of my car and approached him with a handshake and the explanation that he and I would be co-workers. I helped him push the carts across the lot and through the store doors to anxiously waiting customers.

As we entered the market, I saw Baines Spivington working the liquor desk. I bid Ricky a "See ya later," and approached Baines to ask where Harold Chanaga might be found. I gave him my name, told him about the job offer, and mentioned that his brother was a friend of mine from school. Baines grasped my hand across the counter, shook it in a manly style, smiled, and congratulated me on becoming a Ralphs' employee. He directed me to the manager's office upstairs and asked Gladys Shiller, a possibly sixty-something box girl, to take me there.

Harold Chanaga gave me a brief congratulatory talk, indicated I would start work that afternoon, and then sent me to the break room to fill out work-related papers. I was a bit nervous. I had planned to spend the evening putting a dent in the assigned readings from my professors, and here I was faced with the possibility of falling behind as early as the first day.

When I was nearly finished with the paperwork, I heard Harold Chanaga's voice over the P.A. calling for my friend, Ricky, to come to his office. Gladys had stayed with me and was under orders from the manager to get me an apron and show me the ropes of my new job after the paperwork was done. As she took me downstairs, in route to the front of the store, Ricky passed us, going up the stairs to the manager's office. He had a worried look on his face and didn't speak to either of us.

Once we arrived at the front, Gladys put me to work bagging groceries for a young-looking gray-haired cashier by the name of Hilda Bromley. Gladys was an expert teacher, showing me that eggs did not rest under canned goods in a grocery bag, for example. Hilda hit each key on the cash register with perfect precision as I perfected what Gladys had told and shown me with many years of experience behind her.

When Baines Spivington took over the till from Hilda, who had earned her break, it was the beginning of a friendship between Baines and me that would last for forty-two years.

As Baines wailed away on the keys of the NCR in front of him, he asked, "So, Rick … you do go by Rick?"

I nodded my head and answered yes.

"Your dad's not the Jerry Hulse I read every Sunday in the *Times* travel section is he?"

"He sure is," I proudly responded with a thumbs-up and a smile.

"Well, you know, my mom and stepfather use his articles as a guide for their travels. In fact their travel agent knows your dad. His name is Burt Hemphill."

"You got to be kidding me. Hemphill! That's a household name at my house. My dad and mom have known him for years. In fact my mom and dad and Burt and his wife go out to dinner regularly and go to the ASTA parties and awards ceremonies together." (My dad had won many travel writing awards, and ASTA was one of many organizations that had awarded him often for his travel writing.)

Our conversation stopped abruptly when Harold Chanaga appeared at the front of the store and stared our way with threatening "stop talking" eyes. I knew I didn't want to get fired on my first day on the job.

As Baines continued to check out customers, and I continued to bag groceries, Harold Chanaga reached into the manager's booth and pulled out a gray suit coat. It was evident the day was over for him, and even though it was still summer, Harold put on the coat. Meanwhile, my friend Ricky rushed past Baines and me without his apron, and without a word to us he exited the supermarket.

I asked Baines, "What's up with Ricky?" Baines shrugged shoulders his as if to say he didn't know.

Harold Chanaga followed Ricky's exit and traveled across the parking lot to his car. He slowly creeped out of the parking lot and then sped south on Lankershim Boulevard, ending another day of years of loyalty to the Ralphs Grocery Company.

Just as Baines and I were resuming our work and our conversation, Gladys approached us with a wrinkled, worried look on her face.

"Chanaga fired Ricky!" she blurted. "Don Pickles the liquor clerk caught him drinking beer in the cooler just after he clocked in today. I liked the kid, but how … how stupid can he be?"

When we met her announcement with silence, Gladys continued with a look of disgust. "Isn't he a friend of yours, Hulse? You come to a new job and say you and he are going to work together, and wham, you take over for the stupid fired kid!"

Baines and I looked at Gladys and then at each other again in silence. Gladys calmly walked away to another check stand and snapped open a large paper bag. Baines worked the cash register for another hour until his shift ended at 8:00 p.m., and I remained at my new job until closing time at 10:00 p.m.

When I arrived home, my mother was watching the news. I told her about me replacing my fired friend Ricky and what work had been like. She was sad to hear the bad part of this news, she said, but was glad I had a job. Then she went into the bedroom to sleep. I tried reading my psychology book and fell asleep with my bedroom light on and slept until morning.

Chapter 11

Not Always a Valley Boy

My buddy Baines was born on April 17, 1944, to Isabel and Leonard Spivington. He was their third child, being preceded in life by two older sisters, Shannon and Jane. Three years later, his brother, Monty, was born. The Spivington family lived in the upscale Los Angeles neighborhood of Hancock Park. Baines's dad was an executive at Universal Studios and made good money. This allowed the family to live a rich life, and no member of the family wanted for much materially. Baines's mother, Isabel, did all of the things the other rich mothers and wives did, fitting in well at social gatherings and school events and demonstrating great generosity to charitable causes with time and money.

But tragedy hit the Spivington family unexpectedly on July 20, 1956, when Leonard Spivington, forty-eight, father and husband, died. Apparently mentally distraught, he took his life by plunging from the thirteenth-floor fire escape of the Capitol Records Building in Hollywood. (Baines rarely touched on this tragedy over the years I knew him. How it affected his life is a mystery I am unable to share with you.)

Living in the same Hancock Park neighborhood was the Schwartz family. Dr. Ethan B. Schwartz, a world famous pathologist, was the head of the household. He had a wife, Ruby, and two daughters, Marilbeth and Violet. The Schwartz family lived a life similar to that of the Spivington family until a tragedy struck the Schwartz's too, with the death of their family's wife and mother. (Several times over the years, Baines shared with me that her abuse of alcohol was an apparent major contributor to her death.)

These two families knew one another, and after each family's loss, a substantial period of mourning followed. When she was ready, Isabel was very careful in selecting a suitor, and she did not realize that under her nose, in the same neighborhood, was the man with whom she would dance, enjoy fine dining, and attend many theatrical and musical events for the rest of her life. But it finally came to pass that Isabel and Ethan married, bringing their two families together as one.

I am short on details, but I know that the Spivington family moved to the San Fernando Valley sometime in the mid '60s before the nuptials occurred. I found out early in my friendship with Baines that they lived on the same street as my grandmother, Valley Spring Lane in North Hollywood.

When Isabel and Ethan married, they established roots in their first home together, the aforementioned Casa de la Puerta Roja in Studio City. Baines first attended Campbell Hall, an exclusive valley school, and then North Hollywood High School, from where he graduated. He would attend Valley College, San Fernando Valley State College/CSUN, and Cal State Los Angeles. Violet was in the same grade as Monty and me and attended Walter Reed Junior High with us and North Hollywood High School. Monty and I attended CSUN after high school.

The Spivington girls were out of the house and each would marry twice and bear children. Marilbeth Schwartz would marry once and divorce and have no children. Violet Schwartz attended college in Michigan. She became an expert on major world health issues while in college, and after graduation, she traveled the globe earning money as a lecturer on topics from AIDS to toxic shock syndrome.

Isabel and Ethan had two more houses during their marriage—one in the Hollywood Hills and one above Mulholland Drive in the exclusive community of Bel Air. Just down the road from their home in Bel Air lived UCLA philosophy professor, Donald Kalish, who was an avid Viet Nam anti-war activist who also hired the controversial Marxist Angela Davis onto the UCLA faculty. Wilt Chamberlin, the iconic college and professional basketball star, lived in the hills above Ethan's and Isabel's place. His large house was located beyond a gate covered with spears, shields, and ornaments characteristic of an African tribal motif.

Kalish shared martinis with Isabel and Ethan from time to time at their houses. Wilt enthusiastically waved at everyone in the neighborhood when he left his compound and scooted about canyon roads in his late model VW van.

Other than these two colorful characters, Ethan and Isabel enjoyed being surrounded by nature. In particular, Isabel was fond of the regular visits by squirrels and deer in the backyard. Neither she nor Ethan were fond of the raccoons who regularly wreaked havoc at night, knocking over garbage cans containing scraps from their evening meal. Baines, of course, made regular visits to his parents' house to join them for dinner, tend to their needs, or lie by the pool.

None of the kids lived with Ethan and Isabel after they moved from La Casa. Baines was a renter most of his life until the purchase of his condo.

CHAPTER 12

Let the Partying Begin

Not long after I met Baines at Ralphs Lankershim, I became a member of the Beck Avenue Bunch. That's what I called it, at least. My friends and I gathered many times in bunches with Baines and Monty at their house on Beck Avenue in Studio City—La Casa de la Puerta Roja—for activities that did not warrant close scrutiny from their parents. Isabel and Ethan were liberal thinkers and livers. We did things at La Casa our own parents wouldn't allow, such as underage drinking of alcohol.

Baines and Monty had La Casa to themselves many days and weeks at a time because of their parents' travels. Some of it was connected to Ethan's profession as a doctor—conventions, lectures, and professional awards. The remainder of their travels were for pleasure; they enjoyed spending their money on elegant expensive vacations.

Violet was the youngest of three remaining children in the house. She didn't seem too affected by her parents' travels. She was independent in both her actions and her thinking, and she handled being alone with her two stepbrothers by basically ignoring them.

La Casa de la Puerta Roja was were each of the famous Spivy Bashes took place—the parties named by Baines's buddies from high school. As I have mentioned before, Baines was a local icon or idol. The Bashes were another of the premier reasons for Baines's status, beside the car, sleeping with his girlfriend, and having money to spend on various pleasures. These parties were the pinnacle of San Fernando Valley end of summer parties.

I attended my first bash several weeks after I met Baines at Ralphs. He generously said I could invite any of my friends if they were *cool*—a new term introduced to me by Baines.

When he invited me, I was more than happy to help Baines set up for his party. It took us two days with the help of his girlfriend, Cathy, to prepare for this well-attended alcohol-ingesting event. In order to give justice to a Spivy Bash, I wish to share the one I experienced at the end of that summer in September 1965.

The evening of the party arrived. It was a Saturday. Ethan and Isabel were away. The weather was warm. The beer resting in ice chests was cold. Partygoers were beginning to arrive and were anxious to rip up. In the backyard of La Casa de la Puerta Roja there was a swimming pool fifteen feet wide by thirty-six feet long for those who wished to swim in its eighty-five-degree turquoise water.

A stereo was set up in the room next to Baines's bedroom, off from the garage, and there were dual stereophonic Bose speakers hooked up both inside and outside to help rock the party on.

Chinese paper lanterns were strung around the perimeter of the backyard and were supported by well-worn bamboo poles that the Spivington family had stuck in the ground at their parties in Hancock Park. The tiny battery-lighted bulbs inside the lanterns provided subtle light. In addition, a floodlight was attached to the roof of the garage to allow guests to see across the expansive backyard when night fell.

The dress was Hawaiian. It had been for every Spivy Bash since its inception three years before. Most of the guys wore aloha shirts with shorts and tennies. A few wore lava-lavas with no shirt, as did some of the girls, but with a complementing bikini top. Most of the ladies chose to wear lovely flower-patterned muumuus and thongs on their feet. Some were barefoot.

Baines's girlfriend Cathy wore a muumuu that partially covered her obvious bra-less breasts. Baines wore a Reyn Spooner aloha shirt his mother had purchased for him on her recent trip with Ethan to the Hawaiian Islands and a pair of white sans belt shorts. He wore no footwear. (Baines felt comfortable going barefoot, and this would be a lifelong habit when the weather or situation permitted.)

The party began with a bang with the playing of *Wooly Bully* by Sam the Sham and the Pharaohs. Cathy was in charge of the music. Blasting speakers in the room off Baines's bedroom challenged the potential future hearing loss of those who chose to enter the room and remain there.

Outside, the potential for a disturbing-the-peace complaint became apparent to Baines after he received several irate phone calls from neighbors. He asked Cathy to turn down the volume, which she did reluctantly while shouting several vulgar expletives aimed at the complaining neighbors.

Following Sam the Sham, Cathy played Shirley Ellis's hit song, *The Name Game*.

Just a few seconds into the song, the disapproval of the party audience was vividly expressed with shouts, "Turn that piece of shit off!"

Cathy countered with music that would please the partygoers the remainder of the evening. *Lover's Concerto* by The Toys was followed by *Help Me Rhonda* by the Beach Boys. The night's music featured the major forces of American rock 'n' roll music in 1965: *1-2-3* by Len Barry; *I Got You Babe* by Sonny and Cher; *You've Lost That Lovin' Feelin'* by the Righteous Brothers; *This Diamond Ring* by Gary Lewis and the Playboys; Barry McGuire's, *Eve of Destruction*. These songs, among others, set the musical tone of a party that would ease into the early hours of the morning.

I arrived at the party at seven-thirty, just as the sun was starting its descent on the western horizon. I had finished my Ralphs shift at seven and had gone home and quickly showered and changed clothes. I parked my Corvair on a car-lined Beck Avenue, walked through the Puerta Roja of the Spivington/Schwartz manor, and proceeded through a thick crowd of partygoers to the backyard.

Standing by the pool was my friend and co-worker Dennis Dobber and his girlfriend, Lorna. They were conversing with a cute blonde girl. From afar I checked her out. She had a gardenia resting in the wave of her hair, and she was wearing a low-cut sleeveless white chiffon blouse and a pair of short white cotton tennis shorts. She was barefoot. She appeared to be about five feet tall and looked physically well proportioned. I had no date and wondered if she had one.

I suddenly became nervous as I approached Dennis and the girls. As I was about to greet them, the blonde flashed me a beautiful smile. She was wearing ruby red lipstick on her lips, which radiantly framed her uniform sparkling white teeth. My nerves increased, and I started to feel perspiration bead on my forehead.

Dennis smiled at me and spoke. "Rich, this is Mary. She's my cousin from Ohio." Dennis paused. More H2O on my forehead. Dennis continued with a new goofy grin. "I was pretty sure you said you did not have a date for tonight, and neither does Mary. So how about it, buddy boy? Can you show her around and be her escort tonight?"

I didn't faint but felt like I might. I wanted to fade away, to where, I wasn't sure. I was shy when it came to girls. Heck, in high school I'd had only one date. I finally succumbed to the conclusion that I probably had no choice but to honor Dennis's request and uttered a nervous, sheepish, barely audible response. "Okay, Dennis. I'd love to be her escort."

I learned that Mary had been in California for two weeks and was leaving for home the next morning. She had been to the beach several times with Dennis, she said, visiting Sorrento Beach in Santa Monica. I told her that was where I went to the beach when the surf was flat along the coast. I was in my element as I explained to her that Sorrento was the mecca of the infancy of beach volleyball, which she did not know. I further shared with her that many of the world's best players displayed their skills there, including Ron Von Hagen—identified by history as the "Babe Ruth" of beach volleyball. I told her I had seen this magnificent athletic specimen perform many times on my visits to Sorrento Beach.

We continued to converse about her visit to Disneyland, Grauman's Chinese Theatre, and the Hollywood Walk of Fame. She'd dined on a Pink's hot dog in Beverly Hills and a Bob's Big Boy hamburger in Toluca Lake. She had taken in a Dodgers game with Dennis and his parents and had hit the Hollywood Bowl for an evening of classical music under the stars. She said that her California trip could not have been any better. At this point, I felt very comfortable. Socially, I was on a roll.

Initially, I did not know that besides providing me a date, Dennis and his girlfriend, Lorna, were also providing alcohol for themselves and for me and the girl from the Buckeye state. Lorna explained that she had lifted a 1.75 liter bottle of Myers's Dark Rum from her father's liquor cabinet at their Tarzana home. He was a honcho in the movie industry, she explained, assuring us that a single bottle of booze would not be missed from his extensive stockpile of bottled intoxicants he used to entertain his friends and showbiz clients. Along with the Myers's, Lorna had purchased a quart carton of orange juice and one of pineapple juice, several limes and orange slices, and a small red bottle labeled Rose's Grenadine Syrup. These ingredients were resting on a picnic table near the pool along with a bottle of Club House maraschino cherries, a bucket of ice, four glass tumblers, and a martini shaker. Dennis explained that these were the ingredients he would use to mix an exotic Polynesian libation known as Planter's Punch. I recognized the name and told him that I had heard more than one old lady from the Midwest order one when I was working that summer in the dining room at the Coco Palms Hotel in Kauai.

CHAPTER 13

The Punch of the Planter's

I remember the punch Dennis made tasting both bitter and sweet—a lovely combo—and my lips numbing halfway through the first tumbler of his liquid potpourri. Halfway through the second, my worries that I might not have such a good time with Ohio were beginning to disappear. Mary was still nursing her first drink as I was preparing to ask Dennis for a third. Baines and Cathy were making the rounds greeting guests. Baines, as usual, was doing justice to a Coors can, his favorite brew. Cathy was sucking down a Mai Tai as she and Baines roamed the backyard, spreading hospitality to friends and strangers alike.

When they approached us, I was seated in an aluminum-framed picnic chair next to the table where Dennis had been mixing our drinks. I started to rise to shake Baines's hand and give Cathy a hug. But I was only halfway out of the chair when my head suddenly began to spin. I reversed my direction carefully and gingerly placed my derriere back in the chair. I felt screwed. I was nauseous. I thought I might spew. I had imbibed the Planter's Punch too fast. Stupidly. Worse, I had done it on an empty stomach, having last eaten two tacos and a burrito for lunch at noon at Henry's Tacos.

Baines recognized my dilemma and took quick action to remedy the situation. Without panicking, he asked Dennis to help him take me to his bedroom off the garage. I did not pass out but couldn't walk as they each grabbed me under an armpit and dragged me away from the pool. I felt embarrassed as I saw people spin by me with tumbling heads and bodies. Once inside Baines's bedroom, they eased me onto his bed.

I woke up after sleeping about an hour. My stomach was empty, and my head was pounding. I tried to sit up but couldn't. I stared up at a dark ceiling, wondering how I was going to get home. I knew my parents would be upset if they found out what I had done. My father was away traveling. Would my mother tell him when he got back? If she didn't know, there would be nothing to tell. What would I do? I fell back asleep, and Baines had the answer for me when he and Cathy woke me again later.

"Rick. Wake up Rick."

I opened my eyes feeling almost human again and saw Baines standing at the foot of his bed.

"Rick, it's one in the morning. The party is starting to break up. We've got to get you home. I'll drive your car, and Cathy will follow me in the Chevy."

The next morning, I realized that I had not only gotten home safe but had also avoided an interception by my mother; I had managed to make it to my bed without waking her. My new buddy, Baines Spivington, had saved my ass. The girl from Ohio went back home without my good-bye. I knew I would never consume another Planter's Punch.

I attended two more Spivy Bashes before Isabel and Ethan moved from La Casa de la Puerta Roja to their new house in the Hollywood Hills. Even if Baines had wished to continue having his party, it wouldn't have been the same—La Casa de la Puerta Roja being the ultimate party venue in the San Fernando Valley at the end of summer to... *get down*!

CHAPTER 14

Baines the Reader, Writer, Editor, English Teacher, and Thinker

Baines wrote a master's thesis. He wrote several plays. He wrote short stories. He edited and critiqued stories of his students while he was a teaching assistant to English professor Wallace T. Graves at California State University, Northridge. He edited and critiqued stories I wrote, and he encouraged me to keep writing.

With his suggestion and encouragement, I read many of the books Baines was assigned to read for his American and European literature classes: *Sister Carrie* by Theodore Dreiser; *Henderson The Rain King* by Saul Bellow; *Martin Eden* and *The Sea Wolf* by Jack London; *Studs Lonigan* by James Farrell; *The Razor's Edge* by Somerset Maugham; *The World According to Garp* by John Irving; *On the Road* by Jack Kerouac; *The Red Pony*, *The Grapes of Wrath*, and *Cannery Row* by John Steinbeck; *A Moveable Feast* by Ernest Hemingway; *Rabbit, Run* and *Rabbit, Redux* by John Updike; *Catcher in the Rye* and *Franny and Zooey* by J. D. Salinger; *Lust for Life* by Irving Stone; *The Jungle* by Upton Sinclair; *Native Son* by Richard Wright; *Les Miserables* by Victor Hugo; *McTeague* by Frank Norris; and *L'Oeuvre* by Emile Zola.

Before I read any of these books, Baines informed me that most of the authors are naturalist writers. He noted several are considered to be naturalist/realist writers. He explained a naturalist writer is a writer who focuses on telling a story which is often described as grim and depressing, and a realist writer focuses on telling a story in plain and everyday language. He exposed me to two genres of writing I had heard of but knew nothing about. Little did I know that with his encouragement I was about to become addicted to a wonderful reading mini-marathon which lasted close to two years.

Several of the books were based on the lives of their authors, specifically London's *Martin Eden* and Hemingway's *A Moveable Feast*. *Martin Eden* portrays the struggle of a young author to get his stories published in magazines that paid a paltry one penny per word. *A Moveable Feast* is *a* semi-autobiographical account of Hemingway's days as a burgeoning writer in Paris who hung out with the likes of Gertrude Stein and Langston Hughes. I was so engrossed in both of these books that it was hard for me to break from my reading.

My buddy Baines exposed me to and provided me an opportunity to enjoy a prolonged "literary feast": bad meat in a Chicago slaughter house; ballin' the jack with Dean Moriarty in a Cadillac across country; a young Chicago street thug; a ranch hand named Billy Buck; the Dust Bowl; a white guy making rain for black African tribesmen; Holden Caulfield; Van Gogh's ear; a sea captain by the name of Death Larsen. These were some of my favorite scenes, plotlines, and characters from the books I read thanks to Baines Spivington.

Baines Spivington transformed from a mediocre student who cared little for education through high school and into college, into a student who craved for and digested education. It had taken some time for him to do a one-eighty degree turnaround and realize he could think.

I believe a major change in his attitude and behavior can be attributed to Geraldine Dimondstein, who was one of Baines's professors at Cal State University, Los Angeles. She taught children's art, one of the courses Baines needed to take to complete his elementary credential. This wonderful woman emphasized the positive in her classroom and made every student feel he or she had value. There were no putdowns with her, and if you put out your best effort, that was all she asked. She gave Baines the drive and confidence to believe in himself.

Although he didn't complete his elementary credential, Geraldine Dimondstein encouraged Baines to tap into his creative juices, which he did when he finally pursued and completed his Master's Degree in English. He had become a career student. The more he exercised his brain, the more he realized his intellectual capacity to debate critical issues and critical thinkers.

Baines was particularly fascinated with World War II and watched documentaries such as *Victory at Sea* over and over.

He loved to read *The Nation*—a weekly journal of opinion featuring analyses of politics and culture and the oldest continuously published weekly magazine in the United States.

Whenever I visited him at his condominium, he always emphasized he was behind in his reading of the Los Angeles Times, especially the Sunday edition.

With a great amount of reading, studying, and analyzing, Baines became one of the smartest people I have known. In many of our conversations, he questioned the absurdity of the world's politics, the cruelty of humankind, and the greed displayed by rich people harming others to become richer.

CHAPTER 15

Baines the Thespian

Baines's enthusiasm for cinema, TV, and theater generated his desire to become an actor when he was in his early and mid-twenties. He was a student at Valley College studying physical education when the acting bug bit him in the ass. He had played on the Valley College basketball team with Tom Selleck, who later became a famous TV and film star. After his basketball days were over, Baines replaced them with days spent studying acting and performing in plays. He took lessons from Mary Carver, who had taught many famous television and movie actors their craft.

Every time I visited Baines at his apartment, I was his audience for a new acting technique; his development of a particular accent; or, a new way of expressing and showing emotions such as anger, happiness, or sadness. Many times I watched him manipulate different props as he tried to master minor stunts or present a type of imagery. Every once in a while I played a character and read lines from a script to give him practice when the real actor wasn't around. He usually practiced crying after inhaling a few belts of booze. The tears flowed a lot better with this liquid stimulus.

When Baines wasn't on stage acting, he was behind the scenes doing prop work, adjusting the lighting, prepping an actor with his or her lines, or coaching the actors with techniques he had learned from his acting teacher. Burbank Little Theater gave him his first break in a starring role when a director cast him as the male lead in *Charley Was a Lady*. I cannot remember the plot other than it had a Western theme, and Baines played a cowboy who somehow became the suitor of the title character of the play.

I attended the premier performance of *Charley*, and Baines proved himself an outstanding choice for the lead by speaking his lines flawlessly and receiving a standing ovation during the curtain call at the play's end. He acted before packed houses every Friday and Saturday night during the three-week duration of the play.

That was the last lead Baines had in a play. He was cast in strong supporting roles in other productions, which gained him acclaim from the audiences who watched him continue to polish his craft.

One of the last plays of Baines's acting career enabled him to have a major role. The play was a weird one, with a theme centered on mystical dolls with magic powers. Baines invited me and a few other friends to the second performance after a successful opening night.

Baines told me before the performance that he planned to do something that night that he had not done on opening night. He said he would do it just for me and the others he had invited. I intently watched a play that confused me and bored me until Baines walked on stage for the last time. The lead actor had been talking to non-responding overstuffed girly dolls that were motionless and scattered about the stage.

As the actor bent down and picked up a doll and began to caress it, holding it to his heart, Baines pointed to him and yelled out, "You mother fucker!" at the top of his lungs.

The audience remained silent as the curtain closed and the house lights dimmed, signaling the conclusion of the play. No one clapped.

Baines had a few more roles before he called it quits as a thespian. He tried his hand at playwriting with our friend Norm Johnson before a drunken conflict ended their efforts, one I believe was based on Norm's insistence that Baines continue pursuing a career as an actor.

CHAPTER 16

Baines and Women

Over the years I knew Baines, I know he had serious feelings for at least four women. He dated other girls, but these four were the ones he truly cared about and with whom he pursued relationships. He stayed with one to the point of what I call masochism. The names of these women will remain anonymous. I will cite some of the things they did that negatively affected Baines's life.

I do not think any of the four girls wanted to intentionally hurt Baines. Some of the things these girls pulled on him were because they were young, naïve, or just plain stupid.

One of them cheated on him. She had seen the movie *Klute* with Donald Sutherland and Jane Fonda. In the film Fonda plays the role of a prostitute, Bree Daniels, who frequents bars to pick up men. For some reason his girlfriend found Fonda's character to be attractive, and she posed as a prostitute picking up men in bars for over a year without Baines's knowledge. She was so into the character that she used the name Bree when she introduced herself to men. She is lucky she did not end up dead.

Another milked Baines's use of credit cards and used him as her chief chauffeur and escort. She never offered to pay for dinner or even a drink although she had tons of money. She was married but separated, and she stayed so during her relationship with Baines.

A couple of them played with his mind, giving false hints that their relationship with him might lead to marriage. Each ended up marrying other men which hurt Baines deeply. Baines wasn't a sap. He wasn't naïve. He was just in love. Don't get me wrong–he did have some good times with these women, going camping, to dinner, to parties, and to bed. And several traveled as his companion on trips with Ethan Schwartz.

Sometimes Baines brought on his own misery by his own inaction. An example of this occurred on a summer camping trip to Lake Tahoe Debi and I took with Baines and one of his earlier girlfriends. They drove up ahead of us and were staying at a different campsite. Debi and I arrived late in the day and expected that we would all go out on the town that night, hitting the clubs and casinos. Baines's girlfriend had other plans. She chose to go bar hopping by herself, trying to pick up men. Even during the day, she preferred to do things by herself.

Baines should have dumped this girl, but instead he was overly apologetic to Debi and me for his girlfriend's behavior. He stayed with her quite a while before she decided to end the hurt and humiliation she had bestowed on Baines during their relationship.

One evening Baines and I had dinner at Posto, a fine-dining establishment located on Ventura Boulevard in the upscale neighborhood of Sherman Oaks. Our waitress was a sexy, slender, well-kept brunette who looked to be half Baines's age. (He was sixty years old at the time.) With a smile, she said her name was Helga, and when she asked for our drink orders, Baines smiled back as he requested a Tanqueray martini on the rocks with a twist. I knew something was up based on the expression on his face. He fidgeted with the menu when she came to take our dinner order after delivering our drinks. He asked for more time before ordering as he and she continued to exchange smiles. I had seen Baines like this several times before when around a beautiful woman. I recognized it as love at first sight.

Dinner was pleasant, and when Baines wasn't looking at the food on his plate, he was looking for the waitress. I concentrated more on my food and wondered what Baines had in mind for this woman. Over dessert Baines admitted he wished to ask Helga out but decided he would do so the next time we dined at Posto. I questioned the "we" part, and Baines indicated he needed my support. He said he had a plan and would pay for my dinner.

Surprise, surprise, we were there the next night. Baines called me in the late afternoon and told me he'd had trouble sleeping, because he could think of nothing but Helga. He said he needed to see her. He needed to ask her out on a date. The plan was that we ask for her section. After we ordered drinks, I was to disappear into the men's room allowing him time to ask her out. If he was successful in securing a date with Helga, he would then call me on my cell phone, and I would return to our table, congratulate him on his success, and enjoy dinner. If he was unsuccessful, he said he would join me in the restroom and we would split the scene and have dinner somewhere else. I thought this plan was a bit strange, but I did not share this thought with Baines. I wasn't going to reject a free dinner, and I met Baines at his condo at 6:00 that evening.

When our drinks arrived, I did as I was supposed to. I didn't want to just stand in the restroom, because that would look weird if anyone else came in, so I found a stall. I stood inside for what seemed an eternity. Finally my cell phone rang. I answered it, and a happy Baines on the other end of the line triumphantly shared he was taking Helga out on her day off, which was the next Thursday. I returned to our table to see a confident glowing Baines.

Thursday arrived, and Baines and Helga dined at the Pacific Dining Car in Santa Monica. They followed their meal with a movie at the Royal Theatre in Santa Monica and then had an Irish coffee at Tom Bergen's Tavern in the Fairfax district of Los Angeles. He called me Friday morning at school to share these details of his date.

Friday evening, Baines called me again to share that he had talked to Helga. She'd told him that she'd had a wonderful time and was looking forward to going out again. I asked Baines where he was going to take her, and he indicated he had not yet asked her out for a second date. He thought that if he waited awhile, she might not read him as being too anxious.

Several days passed before I heard from Baines. When I did, it was unfortunate news. He had called to ask Helga out for another dinner date and a movie the day before. But she told him she was back with her old boyfriend and could not go out with him. This was one of many times I saw Baines's hope that "this is the one" result in a quick heartbreaking kick in the balls.

It was months before Baines and I returned to Posto to dine. Every time we planned to go there, he insisted that I check to see if Helga was working a shift. If she was, we went someplace else for dinner. Finally, on a visit to Posto, we learned that Helga had quit and had moved on to work at another fine dining establishment on Ventura Boulevard called Mistral.

I wish to share a short story Baines wrote for Wally Graves's English class. I found it among other short stories in one of the folders Tim Ball gave me the day we salvaged things from Baines's condominium. I believe it mirrors Baines's feelings of loneliness and his desire for female companionship later in life when he lived by himself in his condominium.

Feeling Fine

It was a rainy, muggy, and gloomy morning. The routine of toilet, OJ, and coffee, as usual. Aspirin came into the picture because of the night before. The depression was still there. God, how would he survive? He scanned the two-day-old sports page, which usually set him at ease, but didn't. He read the movie reviews, which made him feel more depressed. There was nothing out there he wished to see. He sat in his easy chair and sipped his coffee as he watched a Bill Cosby rerun on TV. At noon the show ended.

The gray feeling would come in the later afternoon. The clock gnawed at him as he sat thinking how lucky he was, because he wasn't. He wanted Melinda. He wondered where she was. What she was doing? Who was she with? He longed for her companionship but instead played her dime store psychologist, always listening to her love problems. He wanted her but did not know how to make it work.

Even as he became progressively more upset over Melinda, his headache finally started easing. The night before, like most nights, he had drunk too much. He felt lonely, as usual. He went into the bathroom and shaved. He showered and then dressed. He forced himself to walk to the front door. He opened it and stepped out. He was going to be busy. He was ready for action.

Most of the stories Baines wrote focused on his relationships with women and the various aspects of being married and having kids. I know he wished to have a family, but for Baines, it just wasn't going to happen. He selflessly took care of his parents, which was close to a lifelong job in itself; he took forever to complete his education and prepare for a meaningful career. Both of these endeavors prevented him from having a normal married life with kids.

CHAPTER 17

Nuts and a Motorcycle Ride

About a month after Baines and I initiated our friendship, we decided to attend the last Dodger game of the 1965 season. It was Fan Appreciation Day and we were hoping to win a car, or perhaps season tickets. As we were watching the boys in blue warm up and take infield practice, I offered Baines a peanut from a small bag of ABC I had purchased at the concession stand. (My friends and I jokingly shared that ABC stood for Already Been Chewed.) He said he couldn't eat peanuts because he was allergic to them. As a little boy, he said, he had been given a peanut butter sandwich, and after one bite, he began to struggle to breathe. He explained that ingesting any nut caused him to gag, closed his throat, and blocked his airway so he could not breathe. Because of this nut thing, he had to have allergy shots. UCLA was where his parents had taken him to get them when he was a kid. When he reached adulthood, he drove down to Westwood in his '57 Chevy or on his Triumph motorcycle.

I went with to UCLA with Baines quite a few times. We tried to make the visits twofold—to keep him healthy and to entertain us. Baines was a big movie fan, and many times after his allergy injection, he and I took in a flick. At other times, there would be no movie and instead a visit to a local pub to down a few beers and get a bite to eat.

There was only one time Baines and I rode together to UCLA on his Triumph. It was a great Indian summer fall day, and the warm balmy weather dictated that we take Baines's bike. Looking back, I can't recall it being a scary ordeal—the bike ride, that is. We most likely took Sepulveda Boulevard in favor of the San Diego Freeway.

Power Memorial High School in New York City had recently graduated a high school All-American basketball player who had chosen to play college basketball on the West Coast. Baines and I had read about the guy, and we had watched him play on TV for the UCLA frosh team. After Baines's shot, he and I decided to drive over to Pauley Pavilion where this guy played. We had never been to a game there, and we reasoned that if we were to attend one, we would need to know where the parking was; where the ticket sales booth was; the best way in; the best way out—all of the crap that sports nut guys bore themselves with before they go see their favorite team win or lose a game.

We cruised toward Pauley Pavilion from the UCLA medical office where Baines had received his needle-injected antidote. I had been inside the place once while in high school as a guest watching Haile Selassie, the emperor of Ethiopia, receive an honorarium for the giant achievements he had made for his people. I can't remember the year, but Pauley Pavilion was a brand-spanking-new facility.

On basketball game days its bleachers housed the raucous home crowd of the Wizard of Westwood's basketball team. Coach John Wooden's boys played there magnificently year after year, their victories contributing to multiple national championships to the amazement of the collegiate basketball world.

As we neared Pauley Pavilion, I noticed the fall colors of the leaves on the beautiful trees lining the campus walkways and streets that crisscrossed before us. I asked Baines to stop the Triumph so that we could fully study Mother Nature's arbor of reds, oranges, yellows, and browns. As the Triumph's engine idled, and we enjoyed the show, we were both suddenly distracted by something that did not fit in with the scenery. A very tall man was walking on the sidewalk in front of us. We could barely see his head which was bobbing in and out of the tree branches above. He was black and appeared to have a black Afro hairdo.

As the man moved out from the trees and neared a street corner and crossing walk, he stopped and bent down to tie a loose lace on one of his tennis shoes. He then stood up like a tree himself, looked our way, smiled, and calmly asked, "How's it goin' fellas? Nice day isn't it?"

Baines and I almost fell off his motorcycle. It was Lew Alcindor, the All-American from Power Memorial. We looked at each other in disbelief. What were the odds that we would come to Westwood merely with the intention of checking out where this 7'2" future NBA superstar played college basketball and then initially see him in *not-so-plain* sight?

CHAPTER 18

Revisiting the Tickets

Almost two and a half years after Baines passed away, I retired in June 2009. With time on my hands, I now had the opportunity to spend time doing things I had not previously been able to because of the constraints of my job as a teacher and athletic director. I had written some of Baines's story, and I was looking forward to having more time to continue my therapy. I had Baines's papers, which I had briefly examined following his death, and I wanted to reexamine them more carefully to see if they contained information that might be pertinent to his story.

I also had the tickets that reflected many of the ways Baines entertained himself and others. The shoebox containing the tickets had fallen apart from wear and tear, and I had transferred them into a plastic bag. The tickets had traveled with me by car back and forth from California to Colorado.

During one cold, blustery afternoon when I was living in Colorado, I decided it was a good time to reexamine the tickets—revisit some of Baines's good times. I had glanced at them briefly as I had Baines's papers when they first came into my possession.

I took them out of the bag and placed them on the kitchen table and began categorizing and counting them in groups—sports; live theater; concerts; and movies. The few tickets that did not fit in these categories included visits to an amusement park, a historic site, a club, and several television shows. Baines clearly lived actively, had fun, and improved his knowledge of culture, history, and human nature.

Baines loved sports of all kinds and at all levels. I separated those tickets first because there were more of them, and they were easier to identify. I placed them into piles for high school, college, professional, and amateur events. If there was a Guinness world record for attending sporting events in a lifetime, these tickets showed Baines Spivington surely was a contender for that title.

Three tickets I pulled from the plastic bag and placed on the kitchen table were double-folded. I opened them to find the following inscription on each: Royal Chapels Choir and Transepts, Westminster Abbey. I figured that Baines, his mother, Isabel, and his stepfather, Ethan, had most likely attended the event. I knew Westminster Abbey was where most British or English monarchs were crowned or buried. At this holy place Baines and his parents most likely not only enjoyed the singing of its famous choir, but also added to their knowledge of the history of Westminster Abbey.

Baines loved learning from his personal experiences as a world traveler thanks to his parents. It was not until later in Baines's life that he demonstrated the same enthusiasm for learning in his academic college courses, when he began to understand and appreciate learning for the sake of learning.

I have to point out that when I first met Baines, he did not consider himself much of a thinker. But later in his life he became basically a self-taught intellectual. He became a voracious reader of the critical issues of the past, present, and future and welcomed the chance to evaluate them with whoever was willing to join him in a healthy discussion or debate.

Remember Norm Johnson, he was one of several people who helped Baines cultivate confidence in his ability to think and reason rationally about life. Earlier I mentioned the play Norm and Baines wrote, *Plastic Bag*. That play served as the motivation for Baines to change how he used his brain cells for the rest of his life. It's too bad it was never published or produced. It would have shocked any audience.

Tickets show that Baines went to the theater and concerts at least one hundred and twenty one times during his life. Many of the events were evening affairs with Isabel and Ethan followed by dinner at a nice restaurant.

Schubert; Ford; Ahmanson; Dorothy Chandler Pavilion; Doolittle; Mark Taper—these were the major venues that provided Baines, his parents, and sometimes friends the experience of Los Angeles's comedy, drama, and musical excellence.

Matteo's; Pacific Dining Car; Adriano's; Citrus; Marquis West; Bob Burns—these were among the post-theater restaurant choices that I know allowed Baines and his companions to enjoy great cocktails; excellent wine; magnificent starters; superb meats, fish, and fowl; and calorie-ridden, scrumptious desserts to finish off an evening out. Several times over the years, my wife Debi and I were asked to join Ethan and Baines at the theater followed by dinner out.

In 1974 Baines attended ABC's 25th Anniversary Salute to Steve Allen. He once took a harbor cruise with someone to Alcatraz Island in San Francisco Bay. He went to the Los Angeles County Fair, the Will Rogers State Park Ranch House, the Los Angeles Tennis Club, the Pasadena and Glendale Ice Houses. Baines couldn't have been bored.

Athletic events at the Los Angeles Sports Arena entertained Baines forty-seven times. The Raiders and Rams entertained him at the Coliseum more than a hundred times. Dodgers at Chavez Ravine, fifty-eight. Angels at Anaheim, nine. He attended ten Rose Bowls. One Junior Rose Bowl featured Mercury Morris's leading West Texas State football team against the Matadors of San Fernando Valley State College.

There was a ticket to the first Fiesta Bowl. Harry La Force and Baines attended the game. I recall them calling me after it was over. They had consumed a lot of beer, and they told me when they tried to order take-out at the Jack-in-the-Box drive-through, the girl on the other end of the intercom could not understand them because they were so intoxicated.

Another memorable ticket Baines kept was to the Late Night with David letterman 8th Anniversary Special from the Universal Studios Amphitheater dated February 1, 1990. I attended this show with him and Ron Merriman. I remember the details quite vividly. Larry "Bud" Melman lit the Olympic Torch to celebrate eight years on NBC. Tom Petty and the Heartbreakers sat in with Paul Shafer and his orchestra and performed

A Face in the Crowd. Dave closed the show by mounting a horse and rode it off stage as Jerry Vale performed the *Late Night Anthem*.

Baines was in his glory that evening. He, Ron Merriman, and I finished off the evening over multiple Margaritas and Mexican cuisine at Casa Vega on Ventura Boulevard in Sherman Oaks. Unfortunately, Ron and I had to get up the next morning and go to work as teachers. Baines slept in.

UCLA versus USC football games at the Los Angeles Coliseum and Rose Bowl in Pasadena, blue and gold versus cardinal and gold, twenty-seven times.

Wink Martindale's Dance Party at POP—Pacific Ocean Park; Disneyland; Los Angeles Unified School District's basketball, swimming, track and field, football, and baseball championships; USA/USSR Track and Field Meet and USA/British Commonwealth Games at the Los Angeles Coliseum.

Baines, Baines, Baines—you lived!

I need to share with you one more ticket that I found in the box at Baines's condo, transferred to the plastic bag, and then laid on the table with the other tickets. It was a special kind of ticket—a wallet-sized junior high picture of my daughter, Catherine. She had given it to Baines years ago. I assume he placed it in the box with the other tickets because it was a symbolic ticket—a ticket to his heart. Baines had been like an uncle to Catherine and Robert, and they both loved him and idolized him as their uncle. Why would Baines not have included the picture with the other tickets to his life?

CHAPTER 19

Car Story

The '57 Chevy sedan that Baines drove when I first met him was painted maroon and had whitewall tires on all four wheels. The engine was a turbo-charged 283-cubic-inch small block V8. Baines had not bought the car new, but it was in mint condition when he made the purchase from its first owner in 1965. Baines was very proud of his car and made sure it was always washed and polished. Regular tune-ups allowed the engine to run like it needed to—hot on the streets.

Baines did not race the car very much, but when challenged by a cocky accelerator-revving adversary, he was always ready to kick some automobile ass. Baines had a reputation around the San Fernando Valley for having one of the fastest cars on its streets.

Before I knew him, he and his buddies used to cruise Van Nuys Boulevard on Friday nights. That is where many of the teens and young adults spent Friday evenings, unless there was a basketball or football game. If there was a game, after its conclusion, Van Nuys Boulevard was the fans' destination. It was a great place for the guys to pick up girls, and vice versa, and a great place to show off a car. Bob's Big Boy Restaurant was located on the west side of Van Nuys Boulevard about two miles north of the Ventura Freeway. The home of the famous Big Boy hamburger drew great crowds to its dining room and its soda counter even when it wasn't a Friday night.

One night, while I was cruising the boulevard with Baines in his Chevy, a girl pulled alongside us at an intersection where the light had turned red. She was driving a newer 1965 metallic blue Chevrolet Chevelle. Baines recognized that the sedan had a 283-cubic-inch small block V8 like his '57 Chevy. I recognized the driver as Gilda Stratton, the daughter of popular television sportscaster, Gil Stratton. I did not know her as a friend, but I knew enough about her to know that she had graduated from North Hollywood High School a year after I had. She looked our way from the lane to our left, gave Baines a steel stare, and shot three revs of her 283, her foot suddenly heavy on the accelerator of her idling car. Baines stared back, matched her three revs, and motioned her to pull over with us onto the next side street. She gave us a high sign acknowledging a potential challenge—a thumbs-up.

As the light turned green, she shot her Chevelle across the intersection and entered the lane in front of us. She sped ahead of us and made a wild right turn onto the side street before coming to a screeching halt and continuing to rev the engine of her motionless car. She was in the middle of the side street as we pulled up on her right. Baines dropped his window with several cranks of its handle. She opened the front passenger power window and gave Baines another challenging "you're mine" look. It would be 283 versus 283, one block only, the two drivers agreed. They started a countdown in unison: "Five, four, three, two, one, zero!"

She immediately burned rubber, her tires screeching viciously as she smoked us down the victory trail! She was driving an automatic, Baines a manual. He popped the clutch and nearly stalled the Chevy. He managed to sputter forward but stayed back to avoid Gilda's victorious smile as she sat in her idling Chevelle a block away at the race's end. Neither of us told our friends what happened that night on that side street off Van Nuys Boulevard. After the embarrassment, Baines slowly drove us to the carhop at Bob's, and I bought both of us Big Boy combos.

Baines would have several more cars in his life. He would buy three more and inherit two. The first purchase replaced the defeated '57 Chevy—a Pontiac GTO we called the goat. It was red. It was powerful. It looked like an automotive bull with its thick body and lines, and it threatened to blast away any street racers who chose to challenge the integrity of the goat's engine. My favorite story about Baines and his cars stems from a ride I took in this newly purchased two-plus tons of automotive muscle.

CHAPTER 20

A Pumpkin for Debi

The Cinnamon Cinder was a teen night club located on Ventura Boulevard in Studio City. It was one of the few such clubs in the San Fernando Valley during the mid and late 1960s. Most of the popular clubs were in Hollywood and were located along a two-mile stretch of Sunset Boulevard. If a Valleyite did not feel like venturing forth to the Whiskey a Go-Go, Pandora's Box, or the London Fog over the hill in Hollywood, the CC was satisfactory to fill a local nightclubber's needs.

This popular nightspot was run by Bob Eubanks, a popular disc jockey for radio station KRLA. He along with fellow jocks Reb Foster and Dave Hull, the Hullabalooer, were responsible for introducing the Beatles to the West Coast with live performances at the Hollywood Bowl in 1964 and 1965.

On August 23, 1964, I was home sick with a summer cold. I was lying in bed in a miserable state and trying to lessen my misery by listening to KRLA on my portable radio. I lived on Camellia Avenue in North Hollywood, California at the time with my parents and my brother, Bo. I was tuning the music in and out when I suddenly became excited. During a break, Eubanks himself announced that at that very moment the Beatles were giving a press conference at the Cinnamon Cinder prior to their debut at the Hollywood Bowl. I sat up upon hearing this news and called for my mother, who was in the kitchen making me some chicken noodle soup. A few moments later, she entered my room carrying a TV tray with a bowl of Campbell's soup balancing on top. As she placed the penicillin before me, I told her what I had heard over the radio—the Beatles were about one-and-a-half miles from our house.

My mother who was hip with the times responded with a smile. "Dickie, if you don't eat this soup, you are going to have a hard day's night."

It wasn't until a year later that I ventured into the Cinnamon Cinder. Like most of the other teenagers and young adults there, I went with the intention of meeting an attractive member of the opposite sex.

Whenever Baines Spivington and I went there, it was usually after work around midnight on a Friday or Saturday. Eventually the Cinnamon Cinder closed and reopened as an adult club called the Magic Mushroom. As a club that now served alcohol, it became our usual last stop for a nightcap after an evening out of drinking and bar hopping around LA. Eventually the Magic Mushroom closed down and reopened as an adult club called the Point After, which attracted a more sophisticated adult crowd.

One night Baines was off, and I was not. Rudy Ripulski was back from Germany after serving a tour of duty there with the US Army. Although he had been home awhile and had partied with Baines and me and our friends, Rudy had never been to the Point After.

Craving female companionship after hitting a few bars in Northridge and striking out, as a last resort Baines and Rudy decided to check out the action at this new Ventura Boulevard club.

Baines pulled his GTO into the parking lot just as the clock on its dash read 1:00 a.m. Baines, Rudy, our other friends, and I weren't cheap, but when it came to buying beers in most clubs, we chose to limit the expense by downing a few outside in the parking lot before entering. Baines and Rudy did so on this night, too, and to say they were glowing from consumed brews upon entry to the club would be an understatement. Baines would often say after imbibing a bit, "I'm feeling *fine!*"

Once past the ID-checking bouncer, Rudy quickly noticed a beautiful girl sitting at a table near the bar. He approached her with beer-induced poise and introduced himself. She replied sweetly and with a blush on her cheeks that her name was Judy. He asked her to dance as the DJ began to spin Chubby Checker's 1960 hit song, *The Twist*. They danced and talked until the club doused its lights.

The rest is history. They dated for a few months before Rudy sprang the question. After she accepted, they decided that the wedding would take place in October 1971 in Ventura, California, Judy's hometown, at Our Lady of the Assumption Catholic Church. They chose to hold the reception outside in the gardens of the historic Pierpont Inn, built in 1910.

The afternoon before the wedding, Baines and I breezed up the coast to Ventura in his GTO. We were ushers in the wedding and needed to be there a day early to rehearse and ensure we knew our duties before, during, and after the wedding. We had booked a room at a cheap motel not too far from both the church and the Pierpont Inn.

The rehearsal went like clockwork, and with few mistakes and few repeat run-throughs, before cocktail hour we found ourselves sucking down martinis at the restaurant where the rehearsal dinner was being held. Judy's father was not hesitant to let us know that the pre-dinner liquid libations were on him.

Before, during, and after dinner the liquor flowed freely for the wedding party and other invited guests. Smirnoff and Tanqueray made those drinking martinis very warm and happy. Those who tried to match the father learned that he had guts made of iron and that he was a true martini man.

The next morning getting up was rough for Baines and me. We managed some breakfast and thought about some hair of the dog. Our heads hurt. Our stomachs were sour. We asked each other what train had managed to hit us head-on, yet allowed us to survive. We decided against the "hair" and decided to gut out our hangovers, at least until the reception following the wedding.

We rented our tuxedos from Gary's Tux Shop in Granada Hills—the customary black coat and slacks with a white pleated shirt and a black cummerbund and black bow tie. The shoes were the typical shiny black patent leather style with laces. We drove over to Judy's parents' house, where the wedding attire had been secure since our arrival Friday afternoon. Although Baines and I looked great in our monkey suits, the brain cells in our skulls denied us any pleasure in what we saw in the mirror as they continued to grate against one another.

The wedding was evenly well-attended, with friends and relatives of the bride and groom seated in pews across the aisle from one another. Judy looked beautiful as she glided toward the altar. Rudy met her there with a handsome smile and gently took her right arm from her father's gentle grasp. When the priest announced what everyone in attendance was waiting for, and Rudy kissed his new bride, people whistled and clapped.

The newlyweds rode to the reception in a black stretch limo, and Baines and I followed in his GTO. To excite the guests as we pulled into the Pierpont Inn lot, Baines shot a few revs and burned a cloud of black rubber that smelled like smoking tar as it rose from the pavement.

The usual toasting of the bride and groom with champagne opened the reception. Then the guests enjoyed a delicious buffet prepared by the gourmet chef of the Pierpont Inn. The Ron and the Gauchos Combo played music on a portable stage as Rudy and Judy performed their first dance together as newlyweds. Then came more champagne, some mixed drinks, beer, and more gourmet food. Others danced to the combo. The headaches Baines and I had been fighting disappeared as we imbibed as we had the night before.

As Baines and I weaned ourselves off the wedding reception booze and readied ourselves to leave, we knew we had to return our tuxedos to Gary's the next day. Since we had paid for the rentals, we decided to get our money's worth and continue to wear them on the way home. As we prepared for our journey south on the Pacific Coast Highway, the liquor continued to absorb into our bloodstreams and affect our bodies and brains.

Not living in Ventura caused a bit of confusion to Baines as we began to motor. We had come via the freeway, and we were now taking a more scenic route that was unfamiliar to both of us. Just as we thought we were lost, we saw a sign that read, Ventura Freeway Next Left Turn. Baines steered the GTO onto Olivas Park Drive, heading east.

We passed an adobe ranch house on the right. Another half mile up the road, we passed a farmhouse on our left. Beyond it eucalyptus trees were planted in a line extending north as far as we could see. Beyond them on the ground, casting a vast hue of orange, were pumpkins detached from their vines and ripe for harvest. There were big ones; even huge ones.

As the alcohol continued to dull our psyches and Baines continued east, I had a "bright" idea. Why not get a pumpkin to take home to my girlfriend, Debi? After all, she had been unable to attend the Ripulski's wedding because of a commitment to work. Why not at least surprise her with one of these Halloween squashes? The idea whirled around in my mind for a few seconds before I asked Baines to pull over and stop the goat.

"What now, Rick?" Baines asked, semi-slurring his words.

I semi-slurred back my intention. We slurred back and forth until we both determined that my idea was a viable one. Heck, there was no one in sight who could see us or stop us.

I exited the GTO and staggered to the edge of the patch. I spied a large pumpkin that had Debi's name on it. It was resting on top of the rich earth, and I headed toward it. As I closed in on my objective and began to pick it up, Baines began to rapidly honk his car's horn. Half-ignoring this as unimportant, I began to lug the orange beast toward the car.

As I neared my destination, I suddenly saw what had inspired Baines to honk the horn. Two farmers were closing in on us at a rapid run, with soil-altering implements in their hands. One farmer stopped in front of me as I struggled to hold on to the pumpkin. My body began to twitch as I contemplated my death at the hands of this grower of squash. The guy who had chosen me as his victim held a raised hoe and was poised to smack it across my skull. His accomplice went airborne as he neared Baines's car and slammed his boots down on the GTO's hood. Shocked, shaking, and a bit soiled, I looked questioningly at my "could be" killer.

"Put the pumpkin back, punk," my adversary growled with a gap-toothed grin.

He reminded me of one of those guys from Appalachia who did not welcome visitors to their woods.

The other guy continued to stand above Baines on the hood of the car watching him through the windshield, and the shovel in his hand seemed to be begging him to put it through the safety glass below. I obeyed the command and moved to return the pumpkin to where I had liberated it. The farmer on the hood exercised his boots some more and deepened the dent he had initiated on the hood of Baines's car.

When I returned without the pumpkin, he suddenly jumped off and landed on the ground like a cat and motioned me into the car. He angrily told Baines and me that we would be dodging bullets the next time he saw us near his and his brother's property. The gap-toothed one gave a shrill laugh as he agreed with his brother's threat. I got in the car, locked the door, thanked God, and told Baines to get us the hell out of there.

When I returned my tuxedo to Gary's the next day, the salesman thanked me for bringing it back in such good condition.

CHAPTER 21

Isabel, Ethan, and Baines's Travels

Westminster Abbey was only one of many famous and interesting places Baines traveled to and visited with his parents, Ethan and Isabel Schwartz. During the time I knew them, they also jetted across the Pacific Ocean to Japan; explored Egypt's Nile River by boat as it cruised along the shores of a fertile green valley bordered by desert; visited the major cities of Western Europe; hit the Hawaiian Islands multiple times; made visiting New York City a major habit; celebrated Mardi Gras in New Orleans; sunbathed, gambled, and lived the nightlife in Las Vegas; toured Morocco in a bus; dared to venture into the Soviet Union; and made multiple other trips that included not only Baines but also other members of the Spivington/Schwartz family. I had the pleasure of traveling with Baines and Ethan to a few places, as well.

My father was the travel editor of the *Los Angeles Times* during the time that Baines and his family traveled to these destinations. Many times, Baines and his parents referred to articles my father had written about a particular place or asked him directly for his opinion on how to get the most enjoyment out of their travels. My father at times helped them arrange their travels, because he not only had connections, but also was an expert in his field. He was repeatedly recognized and awarded by various travel agencies as one of the top travel writers and travel editors, if not the top, in the country. My father was awarded the Legion of Honor by President Francois Mitterand of France for his many years of dedicated years of service to his readers, the travel industry, and France.

When Baines and his parents arrived back from their trip to the Soviet Union, Baines shared their adventure with my father and me. My father had an ear for an excellent story and offered to pay Baines to write an article for the Sunday *Los Angeles Times* travel section. Baines took my father up on the offer and not only did the article appear in the *Times*, it also was picked up, published, and paid for by other newspapers outside the *Times* distribution area.

Remembering this after Baines died, I went through Baines's papers, hoping to find a copy of his article, but came up empty. I went through my papers and came up empty, too. Finally, I called Rowdy Ralphs, who went through his papers and found the article. He e-mailed it to me, and I realized twenty-three years later that the story Baines wrote was different from the story he verbally shared with me my father and I. What I remember him telling us was something like the following:

Baines did the standard stuff during his and his parents' visit to the Soviet Union, filling their days with visits to museums, historic sites, and the arts, including the Kremlin, Red Square, and the Bolshoi Ballet in

Moscow. He indicated that when Russians heard them speak English, most were intrigued and sought to have a conversation with them in English.

Baines, Ethan, and Isabel, who were used to gourmet American food, tolerated the Russian cuisine. They found most afternoon and evening meals at restaurants offered a variety of vodkas to complement the caviar, soups, salads, various meats, sausages, pies, vegetables, and desserts. Many of the soups contained cabbage, as in the case of borsch. Many of the meats were boiled. The pies were filled with meat and vegetables.

Among the vodkas they tried were the citrus (lemon, orange, and grapefruit) and peppered varieties. Baines pointed out that the popularity of vodka in Russia stemmed from the fact that it did not freeze in the outdoors even in the coldest regions of the vast frozen land of permafrost. Baines also mentioned that he found it odd that the Russian drinking fountains consisted of a faucet and a cup that sat next to the faucet on a platform; fountain users were to drink from the cup and then place it back on the platform. He questioned the hygiene of this practice.

When it came time for Baines and his parents to leave the Soviet Union, they were ready to return and plant their feet on U.S. soil. But as is the case in most countries, they had to pass through customs before leaving and returning home. For Ethan and Isabel this was an easy process. The souvenirs all three wished to bring home passed inspection with no problems. Ethan and Isabel's passports and exit visas were examined and approved, and they were ushered through a gate to their waiting getaway plane. (Exit visas at times were required for people leaving the Soviet Union.)

But Baines! What about Baines? The two customs and passport inspectors who'd freed his parents were not going to let him through. They stood in front of him and stared. They then stared at his passport and picture before examining him again with questioning eyes—and then back to his passport picture again. What's wrong? Baines wondered. What are these commie travel cops about? Why are they staring at me? They inspected his passport picture one more time, and then the pinko cops grabbed Baines by the arms and roughly escorted him into a room away from the customs line. People stared at Baines as he looked back from the room with a wrinkled expression of fear. Expletives were dancing around in his head as his better-thinking-self told him not to use them on his new foreign adversaries. Sweat was beading on his forehead as he tried to figure out why he suddenly was where he was.

As his bullies continued to talk to each other in Russian and look at Baines and then his passport, Baines caught a glimpse of what he believed might be the reason for their actions and treatment of him— his photo was Scotch-taped onto the inside cover of his passport. Baines had traveled the world with his parents and never noticed this before.

Baines listened as his captors spewed Russian back and forth before one finally addressed him in English.

"What are you up to, comrade?"

"What do you mean 'comrade'?" asked Baines.

"You are Russian, aren't you? You are trying to escape … huh, comrade?"

Baines replied, fuming, "You have got to be nuts!" He paused before shouting, "I am an American!"

"How can you prove it, comrade?" asked the other captor in a slow whisper. "Your photograph is taped inside your passport, comrade!"

Thoughts fumbled around in Baines's head as he struggled to make out what was happening. Here, his parents who had a Jewish surname had gotten through the gate with no problems and were probably on the plane sucking down martinis—while outside the airliner, unbeknownst to them, their son Baines was about to be shot for treason for trying leave a country he didn't live in.

Suddenly, Baines reached his left hand behind him for his wallet, which was resting in the back left pocket of his Levi's, and in unison his captors whipped pistols out of their shoulder holsters and pointed them at his head. Baines slowly pulled the wallet out from his pocket and flipped it open in the faces of the ones who controlled his fate.

"Here," confirmed Baines nervously contemplating his death, "check out the picture on the driver's license. It's embossed. It's not taped. I'm from California, for God's sake! California, USA!"

The two comrades looked at the license, lowered their guns, and looked sheepishly at Baines and one another. Then in unison, with smiles on their faces, they laughed. "You can go, my friend. You are free to go."

Of course, this might be a bit of an exaggeration on my part, but this is as close to what I remember Baines sharing with my father and me as we each enjoyed a few cocktails made with Stolichnaya Vodka.

Baines told me other stories of his family's travels as well. For example, the trip to Japan included Isabel, Ethan, Baines, and his brother Monty. Being six feet two in a land where women averaged five feet two inches and men averaged five feet seven inches, Baines and Monty stood out in a crowd. Baines related that while walking alone on the streets of the Ginza, Tokyo's most famous market, shopping, dining, and entertainment district, he could spot Monty easily more than two blocks away over the heads of the shorter Japanese men and women.

Sitting at a sidewalk café savoring fresh-brewed ten-dollar cups of coffee, the four of them learned from their server that real estate in the Ginza was valued at $100,000 per square yard. A friend of Ethan's, who was a priest in one of Tokyo's few monasteries, told them that because of the high value of housing in Japan, it was not unusual for generations of a family to purchase a piece of real estate, with the mortgage amortized over a period of one hundred years.

One day when Baines was riding in a crowded Tokyo hotel elevator, he felt exterior pressure being exerted on his crotch from outside his pants and underwear. As he looked down to find the source of the exterior pressure, a squatting Japanese man wearing thick glasses looked up at him and grinned widely as he released his right hand grip on Baines's crotch. When Baines told me this story, he added he thought the grinning, squatting man had an uplifting experience.

Many years ago while on a Nile River cruise in Egypt, Ethan ordered a bottle of champagne to help him, Isabel, and Baines wash down the tahini and hummus filled pita bread they had been snacking on. He used his credit card to pay for the bottle. He was shocked when he received the bill back home. It cost him $450 by today's standards using what economists call the Big Mac Index.

Morocco provided Isabel Schwartz with a broken ankle when she exited a tour bus somewhere in a desert and stumbled down the bus stairs. I know Baines was with her, but I cannot recall if anyone else accompanied them to the land of the fez hat and the city of Fez.

CHAPTER 22

A Fish Story

When Baines and his parents were away, it was my job to help them out by watering the Schwartz's lawn and outdoor plants; watering the indoor plants and one tree; feeding their one aquarium fish; starting up and running the Mercedes and the Jaguar; taking out the trash; taking out the lawn clippings and whatever else the gardener had cut or swept up; retrieving their mail from the mailbox; and retrieving the mail from Baines's condo, as well. These things I did regularly, and I was handsomely rewarded for my efforts with multiple dinners out with Baines and his parents.

It was during one of their trips to New York in 1987 that things did not fare well for me out west. It was a beautiful, sunny, spring Saturday. I went to Baines's apartment and picked up his mail—no problem. I picked up the mail at his parents' house—no problem. I took out the trash there—no problem. I took out the gardener's stuff—no problem. I went to feed their one aquarium fish—problem! The fish that I had fed on my last visit would be fed no more. It was floating on the surface of the aquarium, lifeless. I did not panic but noticed as the possible cause of the fish's demise a nonfunctioning, obviously non-bubbling filtration system. The damned fish was positioned on the surface water such that any visual contact I made with it, it reciprocated with a dead-eye look back at me. This being a signal negative against many positives so far, I proceeded to the door-less garage that covered the Jag and the Mercedes, which Ethan referred to as the Nazi staff car (a bit of irony, in that Ethan was born a New York Jew).

I put the key in the Jaguar's ignition, pressed my right foot down on the accelerator, and turned the key. The Jaguar came alive as the engine revved awake and idled when I eased up on the pedal. After the Jaguar proved itself, I shut it off and checked on the Mercedes, using the same routine—key in the ignition, right foot down on the accelerator, turned key. Nothing. The Nazi staff car was not responsive. This second negative led me to call Rowdy Ralphs. He was one of two car doctors I knew, the other being Izzy Michaelson. Rowdy was mechanically inclined and could also probably bring to life the dead fish's aquarium.

Rowdy didn't take long answering his phone and was not long in arriving at the Schwartz's glass-enclosed Mulholland manor either. He first went to the aquarium. Without blinking (like the dead fish), Rowdy theorized that the rubber tubes of the pump had broken away from the source of its bubbles. It took him a wet right hand, a wet right forearm, and a few seconds to reconnect the source of bubbles that enabled life in the aquarium. He removed the deceased fish, wrapped it in a paper towel, and then deposited it in the trash receptacle near the garage, where he would attempt the second fix-it of his visit. Wisely, Rowdy had brought along a portable generator to jump-start the Mercedes. Without it, jump-starting the car would have been impossible because both cars were facing inward in the crowded garage. To access the battery and hook it up to the generator, Rowdy had to squeeze along the driver's side of the Mercedes and open its hood.

As Rowdy performed his magic, I decided I needed to call New York and inform Baines and his parents what had transpired. Baines answered the phone as Rowdy made the staff car well again. I told Baines first about the fish, and he relayed the message to Ethan.

Ethan replied through Baines, "I hated that fish! Glad to get rid of it."

Baines didn't tell Ethan anything about the Mercedes even though I reported that Rowdy had revived it.

CHAPTER 23

Vegas Baby!

In 1999, on a trip to Las Vegas for a medical convention, Ethan planned to mix business with pleasure. It was also an opportunity to continue to celebrate his eighty-fifth birthday which he had begun doing several weeks before. Baines was with him, and after the business part of Ethan's stay, they invited me to join them for the pleasure. I flew there versus driving, and Baines picked me up at McCarran International Airport. As he drove the Nazi staff car back to Bally's, where Baines and Ethan had rooms, he informed me that Ethan had tickets to see Siegfried and Roy at the Mirage. I was to stay with them for three nights before we would all motor back to LA, and I figured on the third night, when Ethan and Baines were enjoying this famous Vegas nightclub act, I would walk the strip and check out the lounge acts.

When we arrived at the hotel and entered Baines's room, the telephone message light was blinking. Baines picked up the receiver and pushed the missed call button on the phone. It was Ethan saying he was under the weather and needed us to get him some medicine to calm an uneasy stomach. Baines and I complied, and Baines took the medicine to Ethan without me.

That night Baines and I had dinner without Ethan. We enjoyed Wolfgang Puck's Spago Las Vegas cuisine at Caesar's Palace. Opened in 1992, this restaurant was acknowledged to be the trendsetter in the development of what would become a culinary phenomenon, with an outburst of gourmet restaurant openings in Las Vegas.

The second night, Ethan's tummy had settled, and we dined at Onda Ristorante inside the Mirage Hotel. Ethan had read a review of this Italian eatery and told us that it had been voted the best Italian restaurant in Las Vegas by the Las Vegas Concierge Association. He said that the food was billed as "classic rustic Italian cuisine with American innovations."

The review was not wrong. Ethan, Baines, and I enjoyed the fruits of the doctor's labor as he allowed us to order freely from the pricey menu. Tanqueray Gin martinis; starters of carpaccio; warm Italian bread, and olive oil for dipping; scampi for me; veal piccata for Baines; osso buco for Ethan; creamed spinach with bacon crumbs for our vegetable; and a dessert tray with gooey, crusty Italian pastries to add more calories to our fine dining experience. Irish coffees helped each of us wash down our choice of oven-baked, custard-filled flaky pastry.

The third night was the night Baines and Ethan were scheduled to see Siegfried and Roy. Baines and Ethan remarked that afternoon that after the show, dinner would be room service for all of us. To my surprise, Ethan whipped out his American Express card as I contemplated walking the strip while he and Baines enjoyed the white tigers and Siegfried and Roy. He told me that he wanted me to join him and Baines and gave me his PIN so I could buy a ticket in the lobby of the Mirage. I might have to sit apart from him and Baines he noted as he handed me his plastic.

The ticket cost $90. Ethan was more than generous to me, although I found out when I returned with the ticket that Ethan's and Baines's tickets were free. A magician friend of Ethan's who worked at the Magic Castle in Hollywood had given them to him.

As we walked through the Mirage, Baines shared several bits of Siegfried and Roy trivia. He explained that the theater where we would enjoy the famous act was named after the two magicians—the Siegfried and Roy Theater. The entire theater, he continued, was constructed of 100 tons of steel, 75 tons of it being the weight of the scenery used in the show, approximately the weight of a DC-10 aircraft. The final bit of Siegfried and Roy trivia was that one show used enough electrical power to light 4,200 homes simultaneously.

The performance we were to attend had a 7:30 start time. Baines's and Ethan's tickets were for a booth stage front, and I would be two booths to their right. Before the show began, Baines and Ethan were sharing small talk with a man and woman seated next to them. The man and woman next to me were silent until they spotted the couple with Baines and Ethan. They commented to one another that it was too bad they couldn't be seated with their friends, who had bought tickets separate from theirs, and waved at the couple seated with Ethan and Baines. Surprised, I told them that the man and woman they had waved at were sitting with my friends. Before the theaters light began to dim, the man seated with me rose from his seat and approached the couple seated with Baines and Ethan. He brought the couple to our booth, asked if I minded changing my seat, and motioned for me to join Baines and Ethan. (This was the second time I had experienced such a seating coincidence with Baines, which I will share later.)

When the overhead lights in the theater began to dim, a dimmed floodlight from the back of the theater quickly brightened the stage before Ethan, Baines, and me. As we focused on the curtain before us, two tuxedo-clad men opened it suddenly, rushed out from behind it, jumped off the front of the stage in front of us, and sat next to Baines (who was to Ethan's right) and me (to Ethan's left) and gave each of us a hug. I was startled, as I am sure Baines was, when we realized our huggers were Siegfried and Roy. They then released their arms from around us, smiled, and shook our hands. Not knowing who was who, I realized when they greeted the audience and introduced their act that Roy Horn had hugged me and Siegfried Fischbacher had hugged Baines.

Years later, my hugger, Roy Horn, would be attacked by one of the white tigers, a seven-year-old male named Montecore who entertained us that night. The event occurred on October 3, 2003, the night of Horn's fifty-ninth birthday. That he survived the attack was miraculous. After a hiatus of more than five years, the duo gave their final show on February 28, 2009.

These two talents entertained more people than any other act on a Las Vegas stage. After they performed for us, we were invited backstage; a meeting had been arranged by Ethan's friend from the Magic Castle. We thanked Siegfried and Roy graciously for a great show and then went back to our hotel rooms to enjoy room service.

I also traveled with Baines and Ethan to Scottsdale, Arizona, where we enjoyed gourmet dining at the Camelback Inn. On the trip to and fro, we stayed at a Hampton's Inn in beautiful Blythe, California. There we "enjoyed" the cuisine of a local greasy spoon. Another trip took us to San Diego, where we stayed at the San Diego Marriot Hotel across the street from San Diego Harbor. Dinner out one night was at the Zagat-winning Grant Grill at the U.S. Grant Hotel in the historic Gaslamp district of downtown San Diego. Zagat did not disappoint Ethan, Baines, or me.

CHAPTER 24

En Route to Europe, LA to New York

In the summer of 1989, I had the chance to travel through Europe with Baines Spivington and Rowdy Ralphs. I did not have the money to pay for the trip, but because of the generosity of my father, I was able to go. Baines had been there several times over the years, and Rowdy was making his second trip to the continent. Rowdy was traveling in Africa and was to meet up with us in Genoa, Italy.

Baines and I flew out of LAX at 11:00 a.m. aboard a United Airlines 747 on the first leg of our journey and would land in New York before taking off on the same jumbo jet for Zurich, Switzerland. From Zurich we would board a commuter plane that would take us to Geneva, where we would board a train to Genoa, Italy.

The trip from Los Angeles to New York was comfortable for me, but Baines's six-foot-two frame did not fit comfortably in the seat assigned to him. For the leg from New York to Zurich, we were to have the same seats.

Many people exited the plane in New York, which was their final destination. As new passengers filled their seats in coach, a flight attendant approached me and announced I had been upgraded to business class. Without questioning why, I accepted the upgrade. Baines looked forlorn; he would remain crammed in his seat while I would be able to stretch my shorter legs. I bid Baines good-bye with a weak high five and walked to my new seat near the front of the plane.

Sitting in the window seat next to mine was a young man who appeared to be in his mid-teens. He looked out of place in business class. I introduced myself and asked if he was traveling alone. He said he wasn't and indicated his cousin was seated in coach. I didn't ask him why he was separated from his cousin but told him my friend was seated in coach, too. The teen asked me where, and I shared the number and row of Baines's seat. He believed his cousin was seated close to Baines and said he would be willing to swap places with him. I asked the attendant who had seated me whether the teen could possibly switch seats with my friend. She said she thought it would be fine but first had to get the approval of the senior flight attendant.

When she returned and indicated the switch had been approved, I walked with the teenager back to where Baines was seated. Next to him, in the third seat on the aisle, was a girl who had not been there when I left. As I started to tell Baines what was going on, the teenager standing beside me smiled and leaned down to the girl and gave her a hug. She was his cousin.

CHAPTER 25

Zurich to Geneva to Genoa

On our flight over the Atlantic, Baines and I enjoyed better food and drink than we would have in coach, and we were both relieved that Baines's legs were not crammed behind a seat in front of him. With the booze we drank, you would think we would have fallen asleep. No such luck. Baines and I were drunk and awake as the 747 graced the tarmac of Zurich International Airport. We changed planes and were in the air a half hour, and then we landed at Geneva International Airport just before noon.

The train station was situated next to the airport, and it took us six minutes to travel the six miles to the Geneva-Cornavin Station. We exited the train and purchased tickets for a second, longer rail ride to Genoa that would leave at 2:00 p.m.

I had a throbbing headache. I told Baines I regretted drinking so much booze over the Atlantic, and Baines shared that he didn't feel any better than I did. There was a bar inside the terminal, and it drew us in. A beer or two might be what we needed to deaden our pain, so we each purchased two and set them on a white vinyl table and took seats on two white vinyl chairs.

Baines reached into the top pocket of his shirt and pulled out a pack of Marlboro Reds. He removed a smoke, put it between his lips and lit it with a Bic lighter he had pulled out of the same pocket. A smoke ring he blew attracted the attention of a young girl seated at a table next to ours. She was alone and had a backpack strapped to her shoulders. She too was drinking a beer and motioned with her fingers to her lips that she wished to bum a smoke from Baines. He got up and walked over to the girl and gave her a cigarette and a light. She sucked deeply on the cigarette, exhaled a smoke ring to match Baines's, and then thanked him with an accent and a sweet smile on her face. Baines invited her to join us at our table, and she obliged.

She was on the short side and had a slim but attractive body, a pretty face, hypnotizing dark blue eyes, and short brown hair. Her name was Lisa, and she shared she was on vacation for a month before she returned to college in Salzburg, Austria. Her accent was not thick as she spoke to us in clear English, indicating her final destination would be the island of Corfu in Greece. We told her our plans, and she revealed she would be traveling with us by train before boarding a tanker in Genoa, which would sail to her final destination. After sucking the Marlboro down to a butt, she asked Baines for a second, which she sucked down at a slower pace.

Into her third Marlboro, we explained to Lisa that we had a language barrier and that neither of us spoke French, German, or Italian, which were the languages of the people in countries we were visiting. She told us she would help us get to Genoa at least, and explained that she not only spoke English, German, and French fluently, but also spoke enough Italian, Spanish, and Greek to get by.

When we got off the train in Genoa after changing trains twice, Lisa had already used her Italian to get us there and then used it one final time. She told a cab driver I'd hailed we would be staying at the Savoy Hotel. Before Baines and I climbed in the cab, we each gave her a hug, and Baines slipped her a fresh box of Marlboros he had liberated from his tote bag.

Without Lisa, Baines and I were basically at the mercy of the cabbie. She had told us he said the hotel was close by, but she did not share how far away. I was prepared for a longer ride than we took. Five hundred yards or so from where we had left our new Austrian friend, our Italian cab driver stopped his vehicle at the curb in front of our destination—the Savoy Hotel. We paid the small fare in lira and gave the driver two American dollars as a tip and a thank you for apparently not ripping us off.

Our accommodations seemed satisfactory to Baines and me. There were two small beds in one large room and one larger bed in a smaller room. A bathroom with a toilet, sink, and shower was located between the rooms, which were connected by a short hallway. There was a balcony off the smaller room that allowed us to view Genoa looking east.

Not knowing the exact time Rowdy would join us, Baines and I left a message for him at the front desk of the Savoy indicating we would be out dining until about 9:30 p.m. The girl behind the desk suggested we dine at a restaurant located at the bottom of the hill from the

Savoy. The name of the restaurant escapes me, but I do remember that it had fabulous food.

We started with warm Italian bread with a garlic-butter olive oil dipping sauce. Tableside, our server tossed a simple spinach and bacon salad with tongs in an ice-chilled bowl, and then he dressed it with olive oil and parmesan cheese before placing it onto our salad plates. Being a big fan of scampi, I was more than satisfied with the succulent garlic butter-bathed serving prepared by the chef. I gobbled up a small serving of the spaghetti marinara that followed the shrimp, and I washed down both courses with a glass of local Chianti. Baines joined me with the same choice of entrees and drank the Chianti, as well. When the dessert cart pulled up to our table, we finished off our meal with the dulce cheesecake, which our broken-English speaking waiter praised as the best dessert in Genoa.

After our stuffed bodies strolled back up the hill to our hotel, Baines and I knew it wouldn't be long before our eyelids became heavy, begging us to put them to sleep. But we struggled against them, deciding that we needed to toast our arrival in Europe with a nightcap.

Having found out earlier from the girl at the desk that the Savoy Hotel had been part of Nazi headquarters during World War II, at some point before Rowdy's arrival, Baines and I stood out on the deck of our hotel room in our underwear shouting out, "Sieg Heil!" as we raised our right arms skyward, but I can barely remember this moment. Rowdy arrived at the hotel at 1:00 a.m., after Baines and I were nightcapped out. Although we were still awake, our greetings for Rowdy upon opening the door were slurred. Rowdy ended his night with two night caps as Baines and I faded toward morning.

CHAPTER 26

Milano, St. Moritz, and a Zimmer

When we woke up the next day, we were surprised that each of us had enjoyed a good night's sleep, although each of us had a hangover. The hotel served a continental breakfast in the lobby, and after each of us showered and dressed, we went down for orange juice and coffee and dined on some Italian biscotti that was sweet with the essence of anise and cinnamon. While we ate and drank, Baines told Rowdy that over dinner the night before, he and I had discussed where we wished to shoot for on the first leg of our European road trip—St. Moritz, Switzerland. The thought of the Swiss Alps intrigued Rowdy, so St. Moritz it would be.

Following our morning nutrition, with bags in tow, we left the Savoy and walked to a car rental agency. After paying for a VW Golf, we were ready to travel north through Italy before crossing the Italian-Swiss border. Rowdy calculated from the map that it would take us about five or six hours to reach our destination. This would include time spent at rest stops, a lunch break stop, and the opportunity to drive through the city of Milan.

As we motored north on the Italian highway, we agreed that the itinerary for our European vacation would be a decide-as-we-go sort of thing. That was our favorite way to travel. We had done this many times back home in California when we took shorter jaunts together by car.

Uscita is Italian for "exit," as in exit from a highway. (In German it is *auschfart*. In French it is *sortie*.) Exit we did when the signs showed we had reached Milano—the Italian spelling for Milan. It was a Sunday, and the streets were nearly bare of any pedestrian or vehicular traffic. It was midafternoon, and we figured most of the residents of Italy's automobile industry, finance, and fashion capital were inside their homes celebrating the Sabbath and enjoying homemade Italian comfort food. We drove the city's asphalt tributaries until we decided the lack of action in Milano on a Sunday was causing us to yawn.

Once we were back on the Autostrada, Italy's main highway system, our yawns subsided as the green Italian countryside whipped by us. When we began to climb beyond the countryside and ascend into the Alps, we were astounded at the intense beauty nature blessed on this fabulous range of mountains. It seemed that around every mountain turn there was a castle jutting out of the forest or resting on a solid base of granite. As we climbed and descended, our ears popped as if on cue in response to the changes in elevation.

Every once in a while, we came upon a village with a single narrow road running through it. At both ends of the road stood a sign holder with a walkie-talkie who controlled the flow of traffic in and out of the village. After we stopped for several minutes to allow cars to pass us exiting the village, we drove through the village and exited at the opposite end of the road.

When we entered the Swiss Alps, we noticed many signs we assumed were advertisements. Curiosity grasped us with the prevalence of wood, metal, and vinyl signs with the words Zimmer Frei written on them, sometimes in all capital letters. Multiple times to the point of mental nausea, we saw these signs without knowing what the hell these two words might mean. Baines indicated the only "Zimmer" he knew was Don Zimmer, a former Brooklyn and Los Angeles Dodger. None of us had ever seen the word frei.

When we were near our destination of St. Moritz, our curiosity about the possible meaning of the words Zimmer Frei was rudely interrupted by a bull who had mounted a cow in our path. The bull was making vigorous bovine love to his female counterpart, penetrating her depths in a not-so-gentle way. When they parted, we three agreed we had spent twenty minutes viewing what none of us knew *bull* about.

When we entered St. Moritz, we noticed that as in Milano, the town seemed to be dead. Even though it was Sunday, we thought this tourist spot would be hopping. When we found accommodations to suit our needs, we asked the desk clerk why it was so quiet. Basil indicated that by this time of year, most tourists had left behind St. Moritz's biking, hiking, mountain climbing, picnicking, and sightseeing. He explained we were in the beautiful Valley of Engadin which was surrounded by the majestic Alps and that the valley followed the route of the Inn River. Engadin, he said, meant "Garden of the Inn" in English.

After our minor local geography lesson, we asked him where we might enjoy a decent meal, seeing that many restaurants appeared closed.

"Try the John Wayne Steak House," he replied with a big grin, exposing his scrambled, malformed teeth.

I think he intended to surprise us with the name of the restaurant, but Baines, Rowdy and I had been around—why not a restaurant named after The Duke?

Our room was located across the lobby from Basil in a hostel called the Hotel Stille. It was a dormitory-type place, but quite nice. Our room had four full beds and a separate, good-sized bathroom with an open shower stall, toilet, and sink.

Since it would be several hours before we joined The Duke for dinner, Rowdy suggested we make a beer run so that we could start our evening routine as we did everywhere we vacationed. Beer? Run? Where could we get some desired amber liquid on a Sunday in St. Moritz, Switzerland? We could have asked Basil, but instead, Rowdy and I decided to do what we had done in the past—wing it! Explore! Make an adventure out of it!

We left the dorm and headed down a street we thought might lead to a hotel and hopefully a bar. A half mile from our hostel, we spotted a small shopping center. Rowdy scanned the site's directory, and I whipped out a Parliament cigarette and lit it with my Bic lighter. Two puffs into my smoke, Rowdy excitedly pointed to our objective. "Bobby's Pub, Rich! There's a pub around here somewhere. It looks from the map that it's located on the lowest floor of this shopping center." I gnashed my cigarette in an ash tray and gave Ralph a smile and a high five.

We started down stairs in a shopper-less center. We were the only people around. When we hit the last floor, a Bobby's Pub sign stared us in the face. There were lights on inside the place, so we assumed it was open. We entered Bobby's and immediately noticed a refrigerator unit against a wall with beer chilling inside. There was another unit next to it containing cheeses, sausages, and bottled waters. We purchased two six packs of beer from a bartender whose name was Swen, then headed back to imbibe some cold ones with Baines.

We took a different route back to enable us to check more of the local color of St. Moritz. As we approached the beautiful Badrutts Palace Hotel, something caught Rowdy's eye. The answer to the question that had bugged the three of us all afternoon. Almost motionless and with a smile on his face, Rowdy nudged me. "Rich. There it is. Something to bug Baines with. It's right there in front of us."

"What do you mean?" I asked with a blank thought in my head.

"A zimmer's a fucking room! Zimmer frei means rooms available, as in free."

I looked at the source of Rowdy's excitement. A glass-enclosed sign to the right of the entrance to the hotel had graphics printed on it in German, French, English, Spanish, and Italian.

"How do you know?" I asked.

"Read the words in front of you, Daddy-o."

I read the English graphic silently and grinned at Rowdy.

We agreed when we returned to the hostel we would piss Baines off as we got drunk, and he tried to guess what we now knew.

Baines was anxious to quench his thirst. The beer Rowdy and I had purchased was a brand named Rulps. The black cans of suds had a graphic of a gold-colored gasoline pump with a gold hose resting outside its holder. When I handed Baines a beer, he noticed the logo and shared that he thought Rowdy and I had purchased the perfect suds for getting *gassed* before dinner.

As we delighted in our beers, we let Baines know that after we purchased the suds, we had an enlightening experience.

He guessed, "You ran into someone we know?"

We shook our heads, no.

"You met some local chicks?"

Head shakes again.

"A prostitute propositioned you guys?"

Head shakes a third time.

Baines quickly knocked down his first beer and asked for another. Frustrated now, Baines asked us to skip the BS and get to the quick of what we had experienced.

Rowdy and I counted down from three then exclaimed in unison, "We know what a zimmer frei is!"

"Okay, what's a zimmer frei?" Baines asked, seeming relieved we were about to answer his question.

"You gotta guess, Baines," teased Rowdy, grinning and leaning his head forward.

"Rick?"

I leaned my head forward, too. "You gotta guess, Baines," I agreed with a grin.

By now, Baines was worked up. "Okay, ass holes. What is a fucking zimmer frei?"

Back and forth, we played with Baines's mind as we exhausted the beer. He was no closer after thirty minutes of guessing than he had been after the first ten in his attempt to determine the meaning of the words zimmer frei. Our torture of Baines could continue without booze, but what fun would that be?

To remedy the situation, Rowdy quick-fixed a possible dilemma. He reached into his flight bag and pulled out plastic packets of Dewar's Scotch he had purchased in Nairobi. They were the same type of plastic packets used for ketchup and mustard in fast-food restaurants in the States, except they were twice the size and were more lethal than pasty mustard seed or vinegary tomato paste.

As he gave each of us two packets to start, he explained that when he was walking the streets of the capital, looking for hard booze, this was the only source he'd found in the city of more than one million people. It had been difficult to buy alcohol, and beer outsold hard liquor two to one, he said. Fruit of the grape, he'd looked for but not found. He told us that only six in every one hundred people per capita in Kenya consumed alcohol, and the legal drinking age was sixteen years.

Rowdy demonstrated the method of consuming the Dewar's from the packet, which was to simply tear off a corner and suck its content. After the beers and two packets each, Rowdy and I agreed to soften the mental torture we'd been putting Baines through. The three of us were starting to feel a bit numb.

Rowdy. "Bainesy, frei means what it sounz like."

I nodded my head in agreement.

"Sounz like?" queried Baines.

"Sounz like," repeated Rowdy.

"How bout free, az in free stuff?"

"I think you're onta something," agreed Rowdy.

"How bout free skiing."

"Nope," Rowdy and me in unison.

"Souvenirs?"

Rowdy and me together again, "Nope."

"Tours?"

Again, "Nope."

"What in the fuck can it possibly be, guys? I gotta take a piss."

Baines slowly made it to the restroom and Rowdy and I lit smokes. We puffed away until Baines returned for the possible finale.

"How bout free cheeeeez."

"Nope."

"Guys, I give up! Fed up with this shit!"

"Your sitting in one," uttered Rowdy.

I add, "It has four walls, a ceiling and a floor."

"Hmmm? Shit! A zimmer is a fucking room? I mean a room? You guys really are dumb shits, ya know? Real fucking dumb shits!"

We each finished off two more packets of Dewar's as our numbing lips looked forward to our meal at John Wayne's Steak House.

We ambled our way to dinner, which was a good thing. Driving in our condition could have been terminal. The grilled steaks we ate were chewy, as if they had been baked. The baked potato tasted as if it had been boiled in water with its skin on. What the maitre d' called a salad bar was a large stainless steel bowl filled with torn lettuce and some shaved carrots. The crumbly, creamy blue cheese I dressed my salad with made one course of my meal tolerable. The wine we consumed passed inspection, too. We ate lovely Swiss Bavarian chocolate éclairs for dessert and sipped cocoa spiked with cognac and topped with heavy cream.

Back in our zimmer we decided to hit the sack early because each of us was still suffering from jet lag and alcohol consumption.

CHAPTER 27

Dachau

During our evening meal at the John Wayne Steak House, Baines, Rowdy, and I decided our next destination would be Munich (München in German). We were interested in checking out the capital city and birthplace of the Nazi movement and the Nazi Party, and we wanted to visit the concentration camp in Dachau, which was a twenty minute car ride away.

En route to our destination, which was four hours from St. Moritz, Baines noted the irony of our choice to visit Dachau and Munich after dining at the John Wayne Steak House. The Duke had a reputation for being a racist, which was confirmed by his quoted statements in an article published in Playboy in 1971, and here we were going to visit the place where some of the worst racial atrocities of the world had originated and taken place.

Before exploring Munich and visiting Dachau, we needed to find our accommodations for the night. After we exited the autobahn in our rented Golf and drove toward the center of this magnificent sprawling city, we found a beautiful small hotel. The Hotel Englischer

Garten was named after the English Gardens, which were located within walking distance. According to the brochure that I lifted from a rack in the hotel lobby, the Gardens nearby had been created in 1789 by British physicist Sir Benjamin Thompson, who worked as a government administrator.

By selecting this hotel, the manager confirmed, we were ensuring that we wouldn't have to drive to the closest local watering hole, which was a necessity for all of our travels together. Our hole this time was the Osterwaldgarte. It was about fifty yards from our hotel and would provide us with food and drink during our two-night stay in a city whose adult population was consumed with consuming *bier*. The hotel manager, a fraulein by the name of Olga, had recommended this beer garden, which she explained in proud but broken English served the best roast beef with fried onions and butter spaetzle in Deutschland. She recommended their Bavarian cream with cherry sauce for dessert. As in St. Moritz, we had a few cold ones in our room before we set out to have a better meal than we'd had the night before.

We didn't know in advance that the menu in the Osterwaldgarte would be in German only. Our waiter fortunately spoke English and helped us pick out our courses. I went with Olga's entree. Baines and Rowdy chose Wiener schnitzel and fried potatoes. Beer flowed into giant steins as we mellowed into dinner.

As we numbed ourselves with the strong German liquid, a man seated alone and within hearing distance provided us with some strange entertainment. He was reading a newspaper with his face buried in its pages. Every once in a while, he would put the paper down and look skyward and yell something at the top of his lungs in what we perceived was German. As suddenly as he would yell, he would return to his paper, burying his face in its script. The man had a stein in front of him, and we assumed that he had drained it several times as a result of whatever was causing him to overexercise his lungs.

As our waiter served us, we asked him about the entertainer. He explained that he had been sitting at the table and drinking steins of beer for the past two hours. He was a regular customer whose wife had just recently left him for a younger man. As long as customers did not complain about him, management was willing to let him stay, given that he was a big tipper and one of the wealthiest bankers in Munich.

The German food outdid the Duke's in this establishment of culinary excellence. (After our trip, I would tell my father to savor the roast beef the next time he visited Munich. He was in Switzerland and France gathering material for several pieces he was publishing in the Sunday *Los Angeles Times* travel section.) We left the Osterwaldgarte drunker than the banker we left behind.

The next morning, we enjoyed a wonderful hot and cold buffet breakfast as we prepared ourselves for our visit to Dachau.

Between 1933 and 1945, 188,000 prisoners were held in Dachau or its sub-camps. Three thousand religious clergy, including deacons, priests, and bishops, were incarcerated there. If you were a gypsy, Jehovah's Witness, homosexual, asocial, or repeat criminal offender, your odds of being placed in Dachau were high.

Jews were placed there, too, and thousands of them were killed and cremated. German doctors performed medical experiments on many of the incarcerated, including high-altitude experiments using a decompression chamber, malaria and tuberculosis experiments, hypothermia experiments, and experiments using new medicines. The result of this testing was death for most of the prisoners.

In May 1945, American soldiers liberated Dachau and its sub-camps, ending the atrocities that had resulted in the deaths of nearly 28,000 people.

These truths we learned as we walked the grounds of Dachau and visited the empty buildings where prisoners had been housed, forced to work, or killed.

A video we watched in an auditorium brought tears to our eyes as it added to, or confirmed, the atrocities that had occurred in these camps. The narrator of the documentary indicated that even though the camp was located a mere twenty miles northwest of Munich, many of the German people did not know that the incarceration of Jews was occurring because of Nazi restrictions on travel and communication.

We did not talk much as we drove twenty miles back to Munich. We dined that night at the same watering hole as the night before after polishing off several steins of beer. I ordered what Baines and Rowdy had eaten the night before, Weiner schnitzel and fried potatoes. They went for the roast with fried onions and butter spaetzle. We chose Olga's Bavarian cream with cherry sauce for dessert.

CHAPTER 28

The English Gardens and More

When I woke up the next morning, Baines and Rowdy were already dressed. It was early for the three of us, but we were anxious to get on with our day. Quickly I brushed my teeth, showered, and dressed. The three of us then left the hotel to take a walk through the English Gardens which were located a mere one hundred yards from our hotel. As we entered the Gardens, I began to read from the brochure I had lifted from a rack in the hotel lobby.

As we walked along the Eisbach River meandering through the largest public park in Europe, I explained that the scientist who had created the park was also a warrior who had spent eleven years in Munich organizing the Bavarian army. I showed Baines and Rowdy pictures in the brochure featuring summer tourists and locals playing "football", throwing Frisbees, riding horses, and playing cricket on the English Garden's turf. One large picture on the back page of the brochure showed a local boy "surfing" on the Eisbach River.

As we neared the banks of Kleinhesseloher See (Lake), a foggy mist was rising and lowering over its glassy mirrored surface. Ducks paddled in and out of the fog, disappearing into and appearing from a ghostly gray. We heard quacks from ducks we could see and ducks we could not see. We were in a beautiful setting in a city that Hitler had made ugly with the anti-Jewish Kristallnacht pogrom in 1938.

In the brochure was a picture of a nearby café renowned for breakfast. I showed it to Rowdy and Baines. They said they were feeling hungry and the pangs in our stomachs lured us to Schmalznudel, which opened at 5:00 a.m. We were the only patrons in this two-story eatery. Fried potatoes, bacon, and eggs over easy, washed down with champagne and rich black creamed coffee provided us with a most satisfying breakfast. I tipped the cook-waiter handsomely, and then headed back with my buddies who were ready to hit the road.

The next few days, we zigzagged in our Golf throughout the Alps, hitting Liechtenstein; Salzburg, Austria; Lake Como, Italy; Zurich, Switzerland; and Lausanne, Switzerland.

One night in Salzburg, we observed a Japanese tourist group leaving a McDonald's as we strolled down a cobblestone street sucking down Austrian *biers*. One member of the group asked Baines to take their picture. As he prepared to do so, he told them all to smile on the cue "Cheeseburger!"

Zurich exposed us to Needle Park, where drug addicts openly and legally shot up what satisfied their endless cravings for a high. Lake Como and Lausanne gave us great views of two of the most beautiful lakes in Europe.

We spent two days traveling in France. In Nice we observed the spectacle of surfers ripping across storm-generated waves in the Mediterranean Sea. Because of the foul weather, the normally crowded nude beaches of the French Riviera were bare. To say Baines was mildly disappointed would be an understatement. Instead of seeing topless women, we had to settle for smelling various fragrances in the perfume factories of Grasse.

The three of us spent another night in Genoa, and then Baines and I left Rowdy and spent our last night in Geneva before returning home. We had our final European meal in Geneva at a Chinese restaurant, because the Mexican restaurant down the road from it was too crowded.

Outside the owner hawked, "We serve whiskey!"

That confirmed that chop suey was a better choice for us than tacos.

CHAPTER 29

Plunkett

Over the years I knew Baines, I had the pleasure of attending football games with him and his family. Ethan Schwartz purchased tickets to University of Southern California football games because he taught at the USC School of Medicine, loved the Trojans, and was entitled to the choicest faculty seats. He also knew the then Los Angeles Raiders' team physician, which entitled him to purchase prime tickets to the Silver and Black's home games. He had four USC tickets and four Raiders tickets. The seats for both teams were located on the north side of the Coliseum, halfway up in the stands on the fifty-yard line.

When Ethan and Isabel were able to attend the games, Baines and I helped them manage their aging bodies from the Nazi staff car in the parking lot to their seats, which were a far distance from the USC student section or the raucous fighting Raider fans.

The Raiders NFL 1982 season was unique in that it was the first year they were to play in Los Angeles after moving south from Oakland. The season was unique, also, because it was shortened to nine games because of a fifty-seven-day NFL Players Association strike. It began on September 21st and ended on November 16th.

The Raiders first game of the season was scheduled for November 22 against the San Diego Chargers and was to be televised on *Monday Night Football*. Instead of watching it at home, Ethan, Isabel, Baines, and I chose to brave the elements and see the game in person. After the game, the four of us planned to have dinner at the Pacific Dining Car in Los Angeles, which would become an institution after many Raiders games.

I bought a program from a vendor and began to peruse it from cover to cover. On the front page was a picture of Jim Plunkett, the Raiders' starting quarterback. A picture of Tom Flores, the Raiders' head coach, covered the second page. The third and fourth pages had action shots of the Raiders famous cast of players—Cliff Branch; Marcus Allen; Lyle Alzado; Todd Christensen; Bruce Davis; Ray Guy; Lester Hayes; Ted Hendricks; Howie Long; Rod Martin; Vann McElroy; Matt Millen; Art Shell; Mike Haynes; and Marc Wilson. These magnificent players and their coach were about to play their first game as the Los Angeles Raiders in the Los Angeles Memorial Coliseum.

Any pro football fan knows that these guys were all legends during their playing careers for one of the toughest, most brutal defenses and one of the most explosive offenses in the NFL. Al Davis was the new general manager. His picture appeared on the back page of the program and showed him standing on the Coliseum grass wearing white pants, a short white jacket inscribed with the Raiders' logo, a pair of white leather athletic shoes, and dark glasses. His dark hair was slicked back in its standard uneven cut. Below his picture in bold black letters were the slogans his players played by: "COMMITMENT TO EXCELLENCE." "JUST WIN, BABY." "PRIDE AND POISE."

Before the game started, Baines and I bought refreshments for the four of us using Ethan's money—beer and hot dogs for Baines and me; hot dogs and Coca-Cola for Ethan and Isabel. Baines's parents had a large bag of salted peanuts they'd brought from home. They had learned at USC games that the brand sold at the Coliseum came in overpriced small bags, and the peanuts were usually marginally stale. They shared their peanuts with me. Baines, of course, had none.

The Coliseum was almost filled to capacity when kickoff time arrived. Baines had brought his portable radio as usual and was listening to CBS Radio football announcers Jack Buck and Hank Stram, who were preparing their listeners with pregame commentary and game analysis. At home viewers would be hearing and seeing the same from play-by-play announcer Frank Gifford and color commentators Howard Cosell, "Dandy" Don Meredith, and Fran Tarkenton.

When the Raiders took the field, the Coliseum crowd went wild with enthusiasm, blowing bullhorns, cheering at the top of their lungs, and sharing stinging high fives. When the Chargers took the field, boos from the Raider fans filled the Coliseum. In unison, Raider fans reacted to the sound of a trumpet with one large, "CHARGE!"

As the Los Angeles Raiderettes left the field and gathered on the sideline for the playing and singing of the National Anthem, a demure-looking, tall, dark-skinned man wearing a white turban took a seat behind me. I turned and noticed him, because he was wearing a heavy dose of West Indies Lime cologne, which I sometimes wore. I believed him to be a Sikh. He gave me a nice "How's it going, sir?" smile, and I saluted him back with my right hand.

As the National Anthem came to a close, and people started to settle in their seats for the kickoff, the demure man sitting behind me suddenly rose from his seat, thrust up his arms, looked to the sky, and yelled out in perfect British English, "Kick ass, Plunkett!"

As those of us around him looked for where the excited expletive had originated, the turbaned one quietly took his seat, smiled, gave a little chuckle, and shaded his eyes with a pair of cool, yellow-rimmed Wayfarer Ray-Ban sunglasses.

Baines stood and turned, smiled, and gave the Sikh a left-handed high five and agreed, "Right on, brutha!"

At halftime, the San Diego Chargers were up, 24 to 7. What the fans had hoped would be a fantastic start to a new era of Los Angeles pro football was being marred by a dismal performance by the Raiders defense and an outstanding performance by the dominant Chuck Muncie and Dan Fouts, who led the Charger offense.

Ethan became fidgety and said he needed a martini. Isabel suggested we leave the game and make for the Pacific Dining Car. I was willing to go along with this, seeing that the Chargers would most likely continue to humiliate the Raiders in the second half.

Sports nut Baines, however, must have had a vision. He suggested we be patient and give the Raiders a chance. His plan was that if after five minutes into the second half, the Silver and Black's famed offense and defense had not shown up, then we would be on our way to sucking down Tanqueray Gin on the rocks with a twist.

An hour and a half later, we were in the Nazi staff car smiling and thanking Baines for his patience and brilliant foresight. The Raiders had not only won the game, but had made one of the greatest comebacks in pro football, outscoring the San Diego Chargers by twenty-one points. Final score—Los Angeles Raiders 28, San Diego Chargers 24.

Baines had an uncanny way of predicting the outcome of most games in most sports he followed because he knew the players, the teams' strategies and coaching philosophies, and the teams' and players' strengths and weaknesses. Baines was sort of a walking sports encyclopedia, as well. The only thing he was better at was movie and TV trivia.

CHAPTER 30

Walks

Baines and I attended many Raiders games without his parents. Ethan had a bum back and eventually was unable to walk. The seats we had made it difficult for Ethan to access his from a wheelchair. Thus, what Baines and I saw live, his parents saw on TV at home in their beautiful glass house above Mulholland Drive in Bel Air.

Many times my son Robert filled one of the empty seats at Raiders games. His friend Ryan filled the other at least once. There were occasions when all four tickets were available to me, because Baines was traveling somewhere with Ethan and Isabel. I usually filled them with myself, Robert, my buddy Ron Merriman, and on occasion Ron's wife, Linda.

During the years Baines and I enjoyed Raiders football, we also enjoyed USC Trojan football. There were weekends when both teams played back-to-back—the Trojans on a Saturday, the Raiders on a Sunday. When this happened, Baines and I would rent a hotel room at the Marriot across the street from USC. This practice allowed us to get a tad blasted at least on Saturday, because we did not have to worry about driving home after the Trojan's game.

Sometimes the games were boring, because the Trojans or Raiders were totally dominant. Other times the boredom stemmed from the Trojans' or Raiders' failure to show up. On such occasions Baines and I entertained ourselves by checking out the USC coeds or focusing our binoculars on the Raiderettes.

Occasionally, both sets of fans were riled up by a health food nut by the name of Gypsy Boots who the Coliseum officials allowed to roam the stadium freely clanging cow bells and climbing up on the railings of TV camera platforms and the top of the exit and entrance tunnels.

The Raiders fans around us were a fairly well-to-do bunch. They had money to pay for the best seats in the Coliseum, and most had season tickets like Ethan Schwartz. They did not worry about the expensive concessions, where the money they paid for a watered-down beer would buy a six-pack on the outside.

Baines and I liked to give names to some of the fans seated near us because of their looks, their habits, or an association with some social or commercial phenomenon. Hair Guy sat in front of us, down six rows and a bit to the left. We gave him this name because he hid the extreme baldness on the front of his scalp with a massive flap of hair that grew behind his crown, which he combed forward and then folded under. His hair-growing magic gave him a better look than someone wearing a synthetic hairpiece.

Dr. Lewis and his wife sat two rows down from us on the aisle. We named him after the principal I had worked for at Dacotah Street Elementary School, because they looked alike. He was a bit on the heavy side, but not fat. He had puffy red cheeks that I believe came from drinking regular evening martinis. His wife was a lovely looking woman who dressed up more than a Raiders game required. Baines would see him every once in a while at a car wash in Sherman Oaks. He had also seen Dr. Lewis and his wife on Waikiki Beach when he vacationed there with his parents.

Sitting directly in front of us at Raiders games were two men employed by the KIIS radio station. A guy in his mid-fifties sat on the right, and a guy in his late thirties sat on the left. The older guy was always talking business during the games. The younger guy was a good listener who seemed to be trying to set a world record for consumption of beers by one person at a Raiders game. Baines and I appropriately named the senior of the two, Mr. KIIS. The beer guzzler, we crowned, Beer Guy.

Baines and I saw several celebrities during the times we attended Raiders' games. Before one game, the bejeweled Mr. T brought excitement to the few kids who sat near us with high fives, autographs, and a chance to handle the gold chains and precious stones hanging around his neck. Fritz Coleman, the weatherman on NBC's channel 4 and sometimes nightclub comedian, made an appearance at one game and graciously autographed Raiders game programs until his writing hand fell off. Jerry Jones, the owner of the Dallas Cowboys, roamed the stands on a Sunday afternoon before a game and shook my and Baines's hand.

The strangest of the fans who sat behind us from time to time was a guy who looked a lot like TV and movie star, Robert Conrad. We called him The Double.

He had the same short, stocky build as the actor, and on warmer Sunday afternoons, he showed it off in a tank top and volleyball shorts. On his feet he wore thongs, which Baines referred to as Jap slaps. Draped around his neck he wore a ton of jewelry that rivaled Mr. T's. This guy attended most games by himself. Occasionally his wife and two kids, a little boy and little girl, would join him for an afternoon of Raidermania.

On a Sunday the Raiders were to play the San Francisco 49ers, Baines had invited Ron Merriman to join us. We consumed a good number of beers outside the Coliseum before we took our seats. Baines sat on my left, and Ron sat on my right in an aisle seat.

As the three of us discussed our pregame predictions, Ron put his beer down on the concrete step beside him. Like clockwork a little kid being dragged up the Coliseum steps by his father kicked Ron's beer and launched it across the aisle. As the liquid intended for Ron's lips bubbled and hissed away on the porous surface before him, I looked at Baines, who was cracking up. He had won our bet, predicting that accident-prone Ron would somehow lose his first Coliseum beer before the playing of the National Anthem. Usually, Ron would kick over his own beer. Through all of the Raiders games he'd attended, he had a perfect record of losing at least one beer per game. This time it was a father-dragged kid who caused him to exit his seat and buy another rip-off Coliseum brew.

When Ron returned from the concession stand, the Raiders had already kicked off to the 49ers. Marc Wilson was at the helm of the Silver and Black, and Marcus Allen was in the backfield to reinforce the Raiders' passing attack with his bruising running game. Just as the first quarter was coming to an end, the Raiders scored the first touchdown of the game with a short five-yard pass from Marc Wilson to Cliff Branch.

As we stood and cheered, the Robert Conrad double appeared from the tunnel to our right and sidestepped across the row of seats behind us. He was wearing his customary tank top, volleyball shorts, thongs, and the challenge to Mr. T around his neck. His chest hairs crowned the top front edge of his tank top until he took the shirt off, revealing the rest of the black forest on his chest and his back. When he sat down, he was breathing down Baines's neck.

As the game progressed, the Raiders seemed well on their way to a lopsided victory. Beer Guy was celebrating by buying and downing a beer with each Raider score. Fortunately for him, there were four field goals after the Cliff Branch touchdown before the first half came to an end. The Double sitting behind Baines came close to matching Beer Guy, consuming three plastic cups of diluted amber. When halftime arrived, both men needed a potty break, as did my buddy, Baines. As the three headed off to the head, I could not help but notice that The Double was barefoot.

Baines was the last of the three to return to his seat as the Raiderettes' halftime show came to a close. Beer Guy had emptied his bladder such that he needed to purchase two more beers to fill it. The barefoot one matched him as if an unknown contest was on.

As I was about to comment to Baines that the girls in silver and black who performed during halftime were hot, he interrupted me.

"Daddy-o, you won't believe this?"

"What's up, Baines? Why do you have that goony look on your face?"

Baines whispered in my left ear, "The guy sitting behind me, The Double, was standing in the stall next to mine in the head. There is piss all over the floor. I look down and see the guy is standing barefoot in the urine of guys before him who missed the porcelain. Then he leaves and walks in more urine as he walks out of the men's head."

"Bullshit!" I whispered back. "You've got to be kidding me?"

"Look, Daddy," continued Baines, "next time the dude goes to the head, you follow him in there and you observe him. He truly walks in urine."

By now I thought Baines had had too much to drink himself. I looked behind him, however, to confirm that the one he said had walked in urine was still barefoot.

Around the end of the third quarter, The Double rose from his seat and headed for the head. I quickly got up from my seat, gave Baines another "Bullshit!" look, and then followed the guy to his destination.

When I returned, I apologized to Baines. I had seen it for myself. When I whispered to Ron what Baines had told me and I had seen for myself, Ron whispered back, "What do you think I am, stupid?"

I told him I didn't think so and encouraged him to check it out for himself the next time the guy went to the head. Ron laughed at Baines when he tried to support me and tell Ron that the guy had uric acid on his bare feet. By now the man had purchased two more beers and would surely need to take a leak before the game's end.

As the final seconds of the game ticked away, the mythical beer-drinking contest between The Double behind us and his adversary in front of us was being won in a landslide by Beer Guy. We counted eight empty cups of beer stacked in his hands. The Double had stacked six on the concrete next to his feet.

When the game ended with a resounding Raiders victory, the loser of the mythical beer-drinking contest left his seat without his thongs. Baines and I encouraged Ron to follow The Double to confirm that this guy indeed was walking in urine. Ron left and returned before he even reached the head.

"You guys are fucking with me. I'll get you guys for this. Just you wait, you stupid ass holes!"

The 10 Freeway was a bit jammed as Baines maneuvered the Nazi staff car west. When he exited, he turned right and drove several miles north before turning left. The post-game meal for the three of us was scheduled at the El Coyote Restaurant on Beverly Boulevard.

The margaritas were cheap, as was the surprisingly good authentic Mexican cuisine. As the tequila absorbed into our bloodstreams, and rolled tacos and chips and salsa tempered our hunger, a familiar figure entered the section where we were seated and sat down in a booth with a woman, a little girl, and a little boy. It was the Robert Conrad look alike and his wife and kids. He was still dressed like he had been at the game and was wearing the thongs he had left behind on the concrete. As Baines and I started to engage Ron about the reality of this guy's habit, we watched as he rose from his seat and walked toward the john. He was barefoot as he entered the door.

Without cuing one another, the three of us smiled and whispered in unison, "He walks in urine!"

CHAPTER 31

Right Hand

I was never a big USC football fan, but when I was invited to a free game, I had no problem going along for the ride. Ethan Schwartz was able to attend many games with his wife, Isabel, because the seats were just off a tunnel and a wide walkway passed in front of them. When Isabel passed away, Baines, Ethan, and I continued to attend games, but our seats were changed to the wheelchair section.

The initial Trojan seats were located in the faculty section. Below them was the section designated for alumni. Every Saturday afternoon or evening of a home game, Jerry Buss and Jeanie Buss would sit a short distance from us without flaunting their celebrity status. One afternoon USC volleyball star Steve Timmons joined the Busses. I recognized him by his trademark red flattop hairdo.

There were of course the usual rich snobs who sat in other seats around the Kings and Lakers owners. They were quite entertaining when the Trojans were losing a game. They would whine and complain and did not have the guts to realize that when the other team was winning, it might mean the "Mighty Trojans" weren't so mighty.

Baines and I attended one game versus Stanford that was so boring and lopsided in favor of the Trojans that we spent the entire second half trying to come up with the stupidest name we could think of for a rock band. The winner—Conga Drum Toupee. Another game versus Oregon found Baines and me on the freeway heading for dinner with the Trojans down two touchdowns with three minutes to go in the fourth quarter. As we listened to the radio, we realized we had made a stupid mistake by leaving so soon. USC scored not only two touchdowns but a field goal to win the game. Instead of witnessing this tremendous comeback, we could only hear about it through the play-by-play commentary of KMPC's Bob Arbogast.

Over the years Baines and I attended Trojan games, we enjoyed the athletic talent of five Heisman Trophy winners. The athletic specimens were O. J. Simpson, '68; Charles White, '79; Marcus Allen, '81; Carson Palmer, '02; and Matt Leinart, '04. We observed the coaching genius of two of college football's greats in John McKay and John Robinson. We attended two Rose Bowls and two Freedom Bowls. Of the four bowl games one stood out from the others—the 1988 Rose Bowl between USC and Michigan State. For some reason the tickets sent to Ethan placed Baines and me in the student rooting section.

As we sat in the car before the game nursing beers, we discussed the fact that we would have to stand during its entirety. We knew it would be uncomfortable, but Baines and I felt lucky that we had tickets. While millions of other people would watch the "Granddaddy" of all bowl games on television, we would be two of the fortunate close-to-100,000 fans who were seeing it live.

Once inside the Rose Bowl gates, Baines and I expertly weaved our way through the crowd of fans to the concession area adjacent to the tunnel leading to our seats. Even though it was very crowded, with longer-than-usual lines, Baines suggested we do the food and drink bit before the game. We purchased the standard hot dogs and Coca-Colas and maneuvered through the tunnel, up the stairs, and across the aisle to our seats.

When the game began, we were surrounded by USC coeds and male students who had been consuming alcohol the night before and were making an effort to keep their New Year's Eve buzzes going. Flasks were being handed back and forth, and a few kids were obviously popping recreational drugs. Baines and I felt out of place except for the opportunity to eye beautiful coeds and breathe in the fragrances which emanated from their sensuous perfumed bodies.

Two minutes into the game, a very short young man side stepped down our aisle and pointed out that I was standing in front of his seat. He showed me his ticket, and I moved over one seat to my left. Baines hadn't noticed our tickets showed we were one seat apart, and the seat the short guy had purchased was the one in between ours. The man was well dressed in a long beige topcoat, and the head sticking out of it had well-groomed, slicked-back blond hair. He wore a pair of Beatles glasses that rested on the tip of his nose. I watched as he immediately seemed to take note of the fact that all of the fans in our section were standing and that even standing he could not see the game. Presumably because of vanity, he chose not to stand on his seat, which might have proved embarrassing. Baines stood 6'2". I stood 5'8". The guy in the middle seat must have been around 5'2".

My conversation with the guy, whose name was Lance, was brief and to the point. He was a Michigan State alum who had purchased his ticket from a friend who was a student at USC. The friend was in Hawaii for the holidays, so Lance was able to use his ticket. He had flown out from his home in Ohio and was staying at the Langham Huntington Hotel, which he emphasized was rated five stars by Fodor Travel Guide.

Here he was, a Spartan among Trojans struggling to see the game. As he pleaded with the people standing in front of him to sit down so he could see the game, he received drunken looks from polluted college kids who couldn't have cared less about his wish to see the action on the field.

Meanwhile, Baines had pointed out a voluptuous girl standing in front of us two rows down. She was blonde and beautiful and had a rack on her that would do well by *Playboy*. As Lance continued to plead with those blocking his view, the voluptuous one turned to him, stuck up her right hand emphasizing her middle finger, and with a beautiful smile, politely shouted, "Fuck you!"

Frustrated, I excused myself and left Lance and Baines and meandered around the Rose Bowl, trying to catch glimpses of a game I could not see in full from my seat. When I did finally return to my seat, Lance was gone and so was the girl who had flipped him off. When I asked Baines where each of them had gone, he just smiled and said I wouldn't believe it if I had seen it myself.

CHAPTER 32

Baines and My Family

When my kids were little, and I told them Baines was coming to our house for dinner, they could hardly wait for him to arrive. When he did, they were at the door, and each of them was ready to grab onto his legs as he entered the house. He would maneuver the best he could, dragging them around as if they were part of him. It was their routine. He was like an uncle to Robert and Catherine. He treated them as if they were his kids and teased them lovingly. He always brought with him what appeared to be a black doctor's bag. Instead of a stethoscope, a thermometer, and other tools of a doctor's trade, his bag contained a pint of Bacardi rum, a can of Coca-Cola, a bottle of aspirin, and a bottle of Benadryl. He needed the allergy medicine to curb his allergic reaction to our dog Frisky, and later our cat, Emmy.

At Christmas Baines would join us to help us trim our tree. It was important to our kids that he be there so they could tell him where to stretch his arms above his six-foot-two frame to secure ornaments to the tallest branches of the tree. This he gladly did as he substituted rum-spiked eggnog for rum and Coke.

Before I was married, Baines sometimes visited me at my parents' house, and if they were there, my mother and father enjoyed Baines's company as if he was their third son. My father enjoyed conversations with Baines that had substance, not shallow talk. He considered my friend Baines to be his friend, as well. My mother took to Baines like his own mother with the same type of warmth and kindness.

Whenever my family vacationed at Crystal Cove in the summer, Baines was always invited to join us. He would come down and spend a few days with us, sleeping in his van at night.

When my kids were young, we routinely camped in Yosemite each summer. Baines and Rowdy Ralphs joined us there several times, and every evening one of them would share the story of Elmer the bear and the other would shout out the bear's name just before dark, which brought our campground to life.

Baines regularly came to our house for summer barbecues. He enjoyed launching Robert and Catherine off his shoulders into our pool as I cooked burgers on the grill. Our kids were exhausted when they finally sat down at our picnic table to eat, and Baines had to struggle to lift a cold can of Coors to his lips because his shoulders were tightened up from overwork.

Baines was an usher in my wedding. He was there to lend our family support when my mother and then my father died. He helped me take care of my brother in his times of need. When each of my kids got married, he was there to congratulate them with loving hugs. Baines was lucky because he had two families—his and ours.

When Baines died, Debi and I lost a dear friend, and Catherine and Robert lost a dear uncle.

CHAPTER 33

Hanging Out with and Taking Care of Ethan B. Schwartz

After Baines's mother, Isabel, passed away, he continued to take care of his stepfather. He was his chauffeur, his caretaker, and his travel companion. He made sure that the liquor cabinet was well stocked with Tanqueray and Bombay gin. He shopped for the foods that provided him and Ethan proper nutrition. He took care of Ethan's bills and his banking. He accompanied him to the finest restaurants in Los Angeles. He went to the theater with his stepfather. In return for all this hard work, Dr. Schwartz paid Baines as an employee of his corporation and assisted Baines in the purchase of a condominium in Sherman Oaks.

Ethan was ninety years old when he passed away. Although he wasn't being paid much, he had continued to work at Cedars of Lebanon/Mt. Sinai Hospital until three days before he died of a heart attack. After Ethan was gone, Baines's life became more difficult. He was the executor of the Schwartz/Spivington estate. So even as he mourned, he also had to make sense of all of the paperwork, including bank accounts, stocks, bills, wills, trusts, and real estate. The value of Ethan's estate had been drastically affected by his health problems and the costly twenty-four hours a day nursing care he had received over the last years of his life. It was up to Baines and the lawyers to distribute what Ethan left to the Schwartz and Spivington family members who survived him.

I had helped Baines take care of Ethan many times. Usually it involved going out to dinner. In order to get Ethan into the Nazi staff car and off to a restaurant, I would steady Ethan's wheelchair as Baines helped him slide into the front passenger seat. Sometimes we three botched it, and Ethan would end up on the ground. He was a tough old bird, however, and as a three-man team, we'd manage to get him up and into the car as we struggled not to laugh.

Wherever we dined, it was a true culinary delight. We hit the best restaurants Los Angeles had to offer. Many of them were located on Ventura Boulevard in the San Fernando Valley. Adriano's, however, was Ethan's favorite restaurant. It was located in a small shopping center on Beverly Glen in Beverly Hills. It served great Italian and Continental food and just about anything you wished to order. The chef, Ueli Huegli, would come out from the kitchen to greet Ethan and Baines and anyone else they invited to tag along. He always had a joke for Ethan and was very precise in how he told it in his Swiss Alps English. Ethan would howl as he congratulated Ueli's efforts to add humor to our evening.

Romano was always our waiter. He was a rather rotund man of medium height who handsomely filled his tuxedo. He politely greeted us with his thick Italian accent and gave us the latest information on what was happening in his life and with the restaurant business. To Romano, Ethan was Dr. Schwartz, or Dottre. Baines was, Mr. Baines. I was, "Hello, how are *you* this evening?"

Gin martinis were always on the table before we could sit down. The bartender would see us enter the front door and race to mix the vermouth, gin, and ice as each one in Ethan's party shook hands with our happy Italian server.

Romano's second-in-command was Mario, who politely followed his orders with utmost precision. If there was a better restaurant staff in LA, you could have fooled Dr. Schwartz. He loved this place. When he was still driving a car, he would drop by Adriano's after work to pick up the take-out order he had made over the telephone before leaving the hospital.

Besides providing great food, solid booze, and excellent service, Adriano's was a great place to catch a glimpse of celebrities. Charles Nelson Reilly was a regular Adriano's patron. Robert De Niro caused an uproar one evening as he sat outside on the patio, impolitely puffing on a cigar that produced a column of smoke which irritated unsuspecting diners inside the restaurant. Larry King, his wife, and kids quietly dined there several times.

O. J. Simpson came in one night to give a diner something. He stood at the table, talked briefly to the man, and then exited without joining him for an evening meal. This was just after the Juice had beat the rap for murdering his ex-wife, Nicole Brown Simpson, and her friend, Ron Goldman.

There were many celebrities who dined at Adriano's that Ethan and most other members of his dinner party did not recognize. Baines, however, had a keen eye for identifying the most obscure actors, comedians, singers, athletes, and political figures. It was sort of a proud hobby he developed by watching TV, going to movies, listening to radio talk shows, and reading various tabloids, magazines, and newspapers.

One night we entered Adriano's and had only Mario to greet us. As tears welled in his eyes, he told us that Romano had passed away that afternoon at his North Hollywood home from a massive heart attack. This devastated our party. When Ueli came out to greet us that evening, he did not share a joke.

It was not long after Romano's death that Adriano himself, the owner of this fine restaurant, died. Ethan's favorite restaurant would close a few months later, only to reopen as a restaurant jazz club without the quality food and service of its predecessor. When Ethan died, Adriano's best customer entered heaven.

CHAPTER 34

The Pact

Simulating the muffled sound of a trumpet, Baines and I called out in unison, "Tah, tah, tah, tah!" After a short pause, we raised our right hands, gave each other a high five, and shouted, "The Pact!"

I know this sounds stupid, but this is what Baines and I did repeatedly one beautiful summer day in August 1968 as we tried to pick up girls at several beaches in Santa Monica, California. We had made a pact that no matter the odds, together our efforts would get us dates. We did this silly routine to boost our self-confidence. It relaxed us and had a calming effect on us. Neither of us had girlfriends. Baines had broken up with Cathy at the beginning of summer for the umpteenth time. I had been flying solo for some time, forgetting when I had my last date.

Almost every day that summer, Baines and I had gone to the beach and failed to muster the guts to seek female companionship. But not this day! This was it! Baines and I were going to get dates! We were going to pick up two girls and wine and dine them into the wee hours of the morning. Hopefully, if we were lucky, we might each score big time. After all, we didn't have to work that day. We had accumulated money over the summer that was burning holes in our wallets. And damn! We deserved female companionship as much as any of the other guys on the beach! The Pact!

Our plan was to seek out the women, do the trumpet, high five, and shout before we approached them, and then charm them into accepting dates with us.

We decided that we would start at Sorrento Beach, the home of California beach volleyball. Although we knew most of the regulars at the beach, we hoped we might meet some girls who had never been to our summer haunt. Most of the girls who came to Sorrento on a regular basis were there to watch volleyball, drink beer, and hopefully latch onto one of the hunks who ruled the volleyball courts. Although Baines and I were athletic, our attempts to be hunks had met with failure. We were better off watching the volleyball games and drinking beer.

After drinking two beers apiece to reinforce our confidence and smoking a half-dozen cigarettes between us, Baines and I were ready to begin our quest for dinner dates. We spotted two blonde girls who had parked their bodies on the sand some twenty yards away from us. They were wearing blue floral print bikinis and had fair bodies. They were closer to the water than we were. We had not seen them at Sorrento before. I told Baines that inviting them to swim would be an excellent way to start a conversation and hopefully get them interested in both of us. He agreed.

We did our silly routine, rose from our towels, sucked in deep breaths, and headed for the girls. As we approached where they lay sunbathing, I started to speak to them but then stopped before I could utter a word. Baines had suddenly darted toward the water's edge and dove head first into a massive wave breaking on the shore. I felt flushed; my tanned skin felt as if it had turned pink. I quickly joined Baines in the retreating water and asked him what in the hell his action was all about. He apologized and said he'd chickened out. I called him a son of a bitch and told him that when we finished swimming in the Pacific, I would give the girls another shot. Then we spent the next half hour bodysurfing and laughing our asses off.

Leaving the salt water behind, Baines and I were ready to give the girls our best shot. As I approached the girls for a second time, Baines seemed hesitant. He stopped and told me he would do the talking to make up for chickening out. I high-fived him and motioned him toward the girls. Standing in front of them, he gave each a friendly but shaky hello and introduced himself and me. One of the blondes smiled and said her name was Shirley. The other girl just sat there with her mouth shut, uttering not a word. She stared away from us, almost ignoring us.

Baines sat down on the sand and started to share small talk with Shirley. I stood there dumbfounded, wondering what I was supposed to do. Finally the no-name girl turned to me and smiled and said her name was Lily. As she did, I saw that her two upper front teeth had about a quarter-inch gap between them and appeared to be the size of two pieces of white Chiclets gum, much bigger than her other teeth. A bit shocked, I tried to be polite and not laugh and excused myself, indicating that nature was calling me. I then headed toward the public restrooms adjacent to the Sorrento Bar and Grill.

When Baines finally joined me back at our towels, he had a defeated look on his face. His blonde was engaged and saw no reason to have dinner with him. Baines, not being stupid, knew why I had left the other blonde behind.

Baines and I decided a change of venue might bring us better luck. Tee's Beach was a quarter of a mile away to the west, and it always attracted a good supply of beautiful women. We gathered our things and headed out on the hot summer sand to our next destination.

At Tee's we did the trumpet, high five, and shout two more times. Two mature-looking women we approached told us they did not date little boys. Two others couldn't speak English. From their accents, Baines and I took them to be German. The language barrier wasn't a major problem for Baines and me, but they were a bit on the plump side.

We headed farther west, not letting failure discourage us. Two stunning women sunning themselves on the beach in front of the Sand and Sea Beach Club just laughed when we asked them out. As we walked away from them, they were joined by two bronzed overbuilt muscular men wearing Speedos.

Finally, at Will Rogers State Beach, two women we tried to impress told us quite adamantly that they were not interested in men. As Baines and I walked away from them, he asked if I had observed the gold band each of the women was wearing on her left ring finger. I told him I had noticed this and that all of the others on the beach were in pairs or in small groups of the same gender. Later we learned that this beach was fondly referred to as "Ginger Rogers" and that it was the exclusive gay beach in Santa Monica.

The Pact! It had failed.

That evening Baines and I enjoyed Mexican dinners and Margaritas at the El Torito in Toluca Lake. Afterward, we each bought a six-pack of beer and a pack of Marlboro cigarettes, then drove to the Pickwick Drive-In in Baines's GTO, where we enjoyed the newly released movie, *Hang 'Em High,* starring Clint Eastwood.

CHAPTER 35

Colonoscopies

A colonoscopy is a measure taken by a doctor to check the inner lining of a person's large colon and rectum for polyps and other growths that may or may not be cancerous. A doctor inserts a scope that has a tiny camera with a lighted lens on the end into the patient's anus, to see inside the large colon and rectum. There is an instrument that can be introduced through the scope to remove polyps or take tissue samples for biopsies. It is usually recommended that a colonoscopy be performed on males and females as they enter their early fifties. A second one is then recommended five years later and at five-year intervals after that. Of course, there are variations among doctors and patients as to how often colonoscopies should be performed.

I have had two colonoscopies, and I had my second at age fifty nine two weeks before Baines Spivington had his first at age sixty two. Considering I was an experienced colonoscopy recipient, Baines sought my advice and knowledge about what it was like to have one's "anal tube" violated.

I assured him that the experience was painless and that the preparation required before a colonoscopy was more uncomfortable than the "anal tube" invasion. When Baines asked me to be his designated driver after his colonoscopy, I did not hesitate to say I was his man. The blessed event was to occur at the Kaiser Hospital campus in Woodland Hills, California, a hospital Baines jokingly referred to as the Kaiser Hilton.

The night before Baines was to have his colonoscopy, he called me on the half hour as he drank the dreaded salt solution, which had been preceded by the ingestion of a strong diarrheic; Baines remarked that his salty solution was not that bad because it had a lemon-lime flavor. I encouraged him to drink as much of the seminasty stuff as fast as he could. I also told him that if he did, the Vesuvius-like explosions from his derriere would hopefully come sooner and end sooner. This process proved difficult for Baines; instead of drinking his usual numbing evening martinis and watching TV, he was engrossed in hitting the toilet every five minutes for a period of about three hours. When the evening of ridding himself of waste concluded, he called me one last time and indicated he was ready to get some shut-eye before the next afternoon's proceedings.

The next morning Baines called me complaining of hunger. He had not eaten for twenty-four hours, had gone close to thirty-six hours without booze, and could not have his regular two cups of morning coffee before his afternoon colonoscopy. Any type of dark liquid could cause his violation to be interrupted and possibly canceled. Both Baines and I questioned the time he was scheduled for his colonoscopy. I'd had both of mine in the morning, and he was scheduled for a 3:00 p.m.

encounter with the Rear Admiral—Baines's name for a gastroenterologist.

I met Baines at his Dickens Avenue condo around 2:00 p.m. The plan was that he would drive to the hospital, and I would drive him home. This, of course, would be after dinner at the Valley Inn in Sherman Oaks, which would be Baines's way of rewarding me for companionship and support before, during, and after his colonoscopy.

We arrived at the Kaiser Hilton at 2:30 p.m. Baines checked in at the reception counter, paid the co-pay of $100, and put his left arm out so that the clerk could secure a patient identification band to his left wrist. We waited silently for fifteen minutes as Baines fidgeted with the pages of a *Redbook* magazine. A nurse entered the reception room and called Baines's name.

He rose, gave her a slight smile, acknowledged that he was Baines Spivington, and turned to me with a thumbs-up. Noticing this gesture, the nurse asked me if I was the one who would be driving Baines home after he recovered from his colonoscopy. I told her I was, and she asked my name and said I could soon join Baines in the hospital prep and recovery room before he went into the operating room for his colonoscopy. She said she would be back to get me in about twenty minutes.

Approximately a half hour passed before I was summoned by the nurse who had taken Baines away. In the prep and recovery room, Baines was propped up in bed and hooked up to an IV. A saline solution was dripping through a plastic tube into Baines's left arm just inside his elbow. I gave him a confident smile, and we gave each other a high right pinky salute. I sat down on a chair near the foot of Baines's bed as he excitedly began telling me about his prep nurse. She was Asian American, had a well-built and well-proportioned body, and had a stunningly beautiful face, he said.

As he finished his description, a radiant nurse approached Baines's bed and melted him with a charming smile. Baines's tongue stumbled as he struggled to introduce me to his beauty. I looked at Baines and thought the usual—Baines is in love. Her name was Hannah. She greeted me with an equally charming smile and told me it was time for Baines's colonoscopy and invited me to wait again in the reception room. As I left, I heard her tell Baines that the pill she was giving him would cause him to relax. Before I exited the room, I turned to him and saw his face turn red and then pale white. I knew Baines was apprehensive about what he was about to undergo. I made my way back to the reception room.

Baines's colonoscopy did not take as long as my wait in the reception room. When Hannah finally summoned me, Baines had been in recovery for just over an hour. She explained to me in route to his room that Baines's doctor was concerned that his blood pressure was quite high following his colonoscopy, so he would be monitored until it returned to normal. If it did not return to normal, Baines might have to spend the night in the hospital. She also indicated that Baines was not yet aware of his condition.

It was now nearing 5:30 p.m.; well into the cocktail hour. When I entered the room, I saw Baines recovering in his bed. His eyes were open, and his color looked good. With a lazy right hand, Baines motioned me to take a seat in the chair at the end of his bed. As I did, he calmly and slowly asked when we could *get the fuck* out of the hospital. I told Baines that it would not be long and that the nurse had said the doctor needed to consult with him before he could check out of the hospital. Baines shifted his body several times as he tried to get comfortable. I could tell he was still a bit out of it. When he'd asked me about leaving, his words had been a bit slurred.

I sat quietly and watched Baines continue to recover from his ordeal. Hannah took his blood pressure three times before the doctor appeared. When Baines's "Rear Admiral" did arrive, he told Baines about the problem with his blood pressure and said that the nurse would give him something that would hopefully bring it down. The doctor made no mention of the possibility of Baines staying in the hospital overnight. The doctor confirmed that the colonoscopy had been successful and that no polyps or other growths had been found in the large colon or rectum.

Before leaving, the doctor introduced himself to me as Dr. Johnson and repeated that Mr. Spivington would be allowed to check out of the hospital as soon as his blood pressure was at a safe level. I thanked the doctor and wished him a good evening.

As Nurse Hannah gave Baines a pill, which he washed down with a glass of cold water, I thought, *Baines will be pissed if he has to spend the night in the hospital.* I didn't tell him of this possibility, nor had anyone else on the hospital staff. I was thirsty and hungry. I knew Baines certainly was. *Come on, pill*, I prayed. *Do your stuff. Get Baines's blood pressure down so we can get the hell out of this place and on our way to the Valley Inn for dinner. I wondered if we should really dine there. What would be best for Baines?* You are supposed to eat very lightly after a colonoscopy and consume no alcohol. Light foods such as vegetable soup and fruit are recommended, and patients are not to consume alcohol until twelve hours after a colonoscopy. If Baines had his way, we would leave the hospital, and he immediately would do the opposite of what was recommended after a colonoscopy—most likely eat meat, a baked potato, and a salad; suck down a martini or two and a couple of glasses of wine; and no doubt finish off his meal with a gooey dessert.

Baines was totally alert and becoming irksome as the clock on the wall ticked to 6:30 p.m. I suggested to him that we forget the Valley Inn, and I told him my reasons. "Bullshit," he responded as he reached for the buzzer to summon Hannah. When she appeared, he did a one-eighty and politely asked when he could leave the hospital. She explained that unless his blood pressure returned to normal, he would possibly have to remain in the hospital overnight. She took Baines's blood pressure three times over the next hour, until it was low enough to allow him to leave the hospital. Baines dressed while I waited outside the curtain that was pulled around his bed to allow him privacy.

It is Kaiser's policy to transport colonoscopy patients by wheelchair to their car once they have recovered from the procedure. When this policy was presented to Baines, he was reluctant to allow this service until he became light-headed and stumbled toward the wheelchair Hannah had secured for him. Hannah and I caught him by his arms, steadied him, and then eased him into the seat. I went to get Baines's car as Hannah wheeled him through the hospital to the drop-off/pick-up location in front of the main parking lot.

Without help, stubborn Baines was able to get himself from the seat of the wheelchair into the passenger seat of the Nazi staff car. We both thanked Hannah and blew her a kiss as she returned with the wheelchair to her duties with the Rear Admiral.

In route to the Valley Inn, our conversation focused on flatulence. I asked Baines how he felt. Did he feel bloated (which was usually how a person felt after enduring a colonoscopy)? He said he felt fine and assured me that going to the Valley Inn for dinner would not end in embarrassment.

Soon we were enjoying Tanqueray martinis on the rocks with a twist; Caesar salads with tiny fish; braised short ribs with mashed potatoes and steamed white asparagus; a bottle of Mondavi Pinot Noir; and raisin bread pudding with a butter rum cream sauce. Baines and I left the Valley Inn with satisfied tummies and minor buzzes.

CHAPTER 36

Yo Ho Ho and a Bottle of Rum

My wife has never had a problem with me accompanying my friends on short trips to the mountains, the beach, or the desert. Sometimes on these trips we favored a hotel room over a tent and sleeping bag. But most of the time, my friends and I opted to take Mother Nature head-on. When we didn't, it is probably because of bears or snow in the mountains, lack of air conditioning in the desert, or rain along the Pacific shore.

During spring break in 1991, Baines Spivington, Rowdy Ralphs, and I agreed a camping trip to Palm Springs was in order. Although we knew it was a major party site for the younger set, I was the only one among us who was allowed to look but not touch. Rowdy wasn't married at the time, and Baines, the perennial teenager, always enjoyed burning out his eyeballs with the sight of bikini clad babes.

We had not made any reservations and were ready to camp or stay in a hotel or motel. We packed the customary sleeping bags, tents, charcoal and lighter fluid, propane stove, and ice chest with cold Coors Silver Bullets into Baines's van.

165

We left at 10:00 a.m. on a Friday, anticipating that three hours later we would be sucking suds at our campsite. Wrong! Every campground we hit in the Palm Springs area was filled to capacity. So we checked the hotels and motels we thought might provide us rooms and beds in place of tents and sleeping bags. Wrong again! The attractive hotels and motels we checked out were booked full for that night and nights beyond. The ones featuring managers with missing teeth and unattractive grounds scattered with trash and cigarette butts were booked full, as well.

Frustrated, we discussed staying with my parents, who lived in Palm Springs; we knew they would welcome us with open arms. But how much fun would we have? For one, we'd have to curb our usual consumption of alcohol around them. With that one thought, we agreed my parents would not entertain us as their guests.

Baines used various forms of the f-word as he drove us around in a continued search for a place to stay in Palm Springs. As our luck started to wane, I suggested we try some other town in the Coachella Valley—perhaps Indio or La Quinta. Baines suggested Desert Hot Springs. It was closer than the other two according to the map Baines was reading, and the three of us had not been there. We agreed Desert Hot Springs it would be.

As we headed east on Palm Canyon Drive toward Desert Hot Springs, a light breeze started to strengthen. By the time we had driven two miles, we could barely see the road or anything else around us because a very strong wind was whipping the desert sand into a cloud of swirling gritty dust. Besides blinding us, the sand was spraying Baines's van in turbulent waves. As

Baines creeped along at a slow but steady pace, a sign barely visible to us pointed to the freeway a quarter of a mile away.

Not wanting to take the chance of the sandstorm stripping the paint off his van, Baines suggested that getting on the freeway might allow us to ride above the blowing sand and eventually outrun the storm. Rowdy and I agreed, and as we entered the freeway, the three of us prayed that we wouldn't be hit by an unseen vehicle. Baines accelerated to the speed limit of 65 mph and kept it steady, hoping a slower car was not ahead of us.

As we approached the freeway intersection that allowed Highway 86 to branch off from Highway 10, the wind continued to blow. A sand-battered sign indicated that the La Quinta/Indio exit was two miles away and that further south on Highway 86 lay the towns of Coachella, Thermal, Mecca, Salton Sea, and Borrego Springs. If we chose to continue east on Highway 10, the town of Blythe was one hundred miles away.

Baines had been there several times and shared that although it was located adjacent to the Colorado River, it had nothing to offer in the way of fine dining and drinking and was basically a redneck, hick town. Rowdy said he had been to Anza Borrego State Park in Borrego Springs before and pointed out that there were basically no limits to the number of campers it could accommodate. It was the largest state park in California, he said, and was famous for its painted desert. Borrego Springs was about the same distance away as Blythe and seemed a better choice for a place to camp. At this point we had concluded that a hotel or motel was out.

Without a flip of a coin, we decided that we would take Highway 86 and shoot for the state park instead of screwing around and wasting time in the other towns along the way. As we passed the town of Coachella, the wind began to subside, and two hours later, we were at the gates of Anza Borrego State Park with not even a hint of a breeze.

Once inside the park grounds, we went to the park store and purchased three rib eye steaks; two frozen packages of Jolly Green Giant Broccoli and Cauliflower in Butter Sauce; a loaf of San Francisco sourdough bread; a pound of butter; two 1.5 liters of Clos Dubois pinot noir; a half-gallon of milk; a jar of Folgers instant coffee; and Cheerios. Baines insisted on purchasing a 1.75 liter bottle of dark Bacardi Rum and a quart-size carton of heavy cream which he claimed he needed to concoct "Caribbean coffee blastos" for each of us at the evening's end. Baines was not shy when looking at the brighter side of enjoying the rigors of camping.

When our tents were up, Rowdy started the barbecue to cook our steaks, and I started the stove to boil water to cook our frozen vegetables. As Rowdy and I sucked beers and waited for our dinner, Baines readied his sleeping quarters in the back of his van. He tediously arranged his sleeping bag, his portable radio, a battery-powered reading lamp, and a coffee can to pee in. Baines had a weak bladder, which had kept him out of the service during the Vietnam War. On his many camping trips, the coffee can allowed him to get immediate relief without having to go to the head late at night or during the *wee* hours of the morning.

As the steaks began to sizzle on the grill, Baines slipped a *Gershwin's Greatest Hits* tape into the van's tape deck. He then lit a kerosene lamp and placed it on a portable picnic table as the sun's light began to sink beneath the rim of the hills and mountains to our west. *Rhapsody in Blue* blared through the sandstone cliff walls surrounding us as the sun disappeared. *I Got Rhythm* and *An American in Paris* accompanied the growing desert darkness.

Beer before dinner was followed by wine with dinner. After two goblet glasses of pinot noir each, Baines, Rowdy, and I headed into the early evening with minor buzzes. Baines replaced the light of the kerosene lamp with the light of a campfire, which he expertly kindled around blocks of dry wood. A third glass of wine each intensified the numbness of our lips and caused us to speak slower as we conversed about the day's challenge to find a place to stay.

Over our first "Caribbean coffee blasto," we decided that each of us would share his favorite camping story. Baines went first, telling about the time he and Cathy almost started a forest fire in Kings Canyon. She was fanning their campfire with a folded newspaper just before dusk, and she accidentally sent small embers flying through the air, which ignited the pine needles on the ground outside of the concrete fire pit. After trying to put out the fire with two one-gallon plastic bottles of water, Baines resorted to using an extinguisher he had stored in his van. Without his quick thinking and action, there might not have been any forest left.

Rowdy related how one summer our poor friend, Harry La Force, was trying to impress a girl he had taken camping in Yosemite. Over the three days they were there, everything he did to make her comfortable seemed unappreciated. One afternoon, when they were hiking in the forest, Harry tried to help the girl down a steep slope. While doing so, Harry lost his footing and tumbled partway down the slope, scraping a great deal of skin off his right shin. Although he did not seek first aid from the rangers, he probably should have. The wound he sustained looked like strings of cooked spaghetti noodles with a red sauce. The girl showed him mild sympathy only. To add *salt* to the wound, she called her girlfriend, who drove up to Yosemite from Southern California and picked her up, shortening her stay with poor Harry.

I ended the favorite camping storytelling with the adventure my wife, Debi, and I had in Sequoia. We were there with a group of my fellow teachers and their spouses and kids. Camping in a tent next to ours was an Englishman by the name of Tony and his two daughters. The girls were from Boston, where they lived with their mother. They had come to visit their divorced father in California over spring break. We befriended Tony and his daughters, and Debi took to the girls like a mother hen. One afternoon Tony, the girls, Debi, and I decided to hike one of the marked mountain trails. During the hike, we spotted a mama bear and her three cubs. They were about fifty yards up the trail ahead of us and caused us to abandon our exercise. Back at the camp we told the others in our party about the bears.

That night over a campfire, Orin, the son of one of my teacher friends, who was usually a wise ass, volunteered to satisfy everyone's sweet tooth and make s'mores. As it grew late and all the s'mores were eaten, Tony's daughters' eyelids became heavy. He excused himself and the girls, and they left the campfire for the comfort of their tent. The rest of us followed shortly as the late night approached early morning.

The next morning, Tony greeted all of us with silence. He had an angry look on his face. I asked him what was going on, and he shouted that some "a-hole" had smeared his tent with s'mores and that bears had visited the outside of his tent, nearly scaring his little girls to death. He showed me the remains of the mess still smeared on the outside of his tent. No one in our camp owned up to the stunt, but months later I learned from Orin's mother that it was he who had committed the dastardly deed.

Blasto 1 was followed by a blasto 2. Rowdy and Baines and I were feeling no pain. A couple shots of straight Bacardi put us in a state of total intoxication. As we gazed at the stars above and contemplated hitting the sack, coyotes howling in the distance seemed to confirm that our evening should come to an end.

When we woke up the next morning, we convinced each other that we had somehow fractured our skulls the night before. Alcohol-induced headaches and dehydration made the slightest movements a monumental struggle as each of us wished for death to take away our terrible pain. Multiple cups of black coffee and bowls of Cheerios and milk did little if anything to make us feel better. Baines popped two aspirins and washed them down with a Coors Silver Bullet. Rowdy and I opted out of that antidote, feeling sick as we watched Baines down a second amber light.

It grew hot as the morning began to work its way toward noon. At 9:30 a.m., a portable thermometer hanging in Baines's van read 95 degrees Fahrenheit. We planned to drive where feasible in Baines's van, but Rowdy pointed out there were areas in the Anza Borrego Desert where only four-wheel-drive vehicles were fit to negotiate the soft sand. If we found ourselves in such an area, we planned to hike, preventing the possibility of Baines's van getting stuck. As we headed out of our campsite, we all continued to suffer from the effects of our previous night's heavy drinking.

We were headed for Hawk Canyon, where some of the most colorful cliffs in the desert are located. Along the way we met a female forest ranger riding in a jeep who assured us we were headed in the right direction. Instead of getting on our way after confirmation from the ranger, Baines proceeded to flirt with the ranger for a half hour before he realized Rowdy and I were getting pissed off and ready to tell his new girlfriend to get lost. By then the temperature on the portable thermometer in Baines's van had reached 100 degrees Fahrenheit.

What we had planned to be a glorious day of hiking through Hawk Canyon came to an abrupt end after only one hour and a half. We unanimously agreed that we had seen enough of desert nature. We needed to rest and get out of the afternoon sun. What water we'd brought with us we had consumed, and another visit to the park store to replenish our supply was in order.

At the park store Baines expressed a desire to have rib eye steaks again for dinner. But instead of frozen vegetables, we agreed to have fresh corn on the cob wrapped in aluminum and cooked on the barbecue. We also picked up a case of bottled water, ice for the ice chest, and another 1.5 liter bottle of Clos Dubois pinot noir. Baines bought a bottle of Tums and a packet of Alka Seltzer tablets, anticipating a repeat of the prior night's booze consumption. Rowdy and I assured him we wouldn't need to share his tablets.

The next morning we were not as hungover as the morning before. We had gone lighter on the booze and consumed more water. Although we were all still a bit dehydrated, we did not have a death wish as we had some twenty-four hours earlier. We decided that the desert was not our friend, no matter the beauty it displayed.

Baines suggested we head for cooler weather and make Oceanside our next destination. He checked the road map and using the mile markers calculated that we were approximately eighty-five miles from our next destination. We slowly packed the van and welcomed the thought that a beach was about an hour and a half away.

Baines and Rowdy sat in the front seats of the van; Baines in the driver's seat and Rowdy in the passenger's seat. I sat in a beach chair at the rear of the van braced between the back door and one of two large stereo speakers Baines had fixed to the van's interior walls. But when we were ready to leave, Baines's van wouldn't start; the engine wouldn't turn over! Try as Baines might, the engine coughed and sputtered each time he turned on the ignition and pushed down on the accelerator. Baines began his customary cursing and began to turn pink and then red with frustration and anger.

A calm Rowdy suggested that the desert dust might be the problem and believed the carburetor might need priming because of all the dust it had collected during our desert drives. Rowdy said we needed gasoline to prime the carburetor. But the walk to get some at the Borrego Springs gas station seemed out of the question as the heat of the day continued to rise; and we had no hose to siphon any gasoline from the fuel tank.

Suddenly Baines presented a seemingly ridiculous idea to us—rum, Bacardi Rum. Why not prime the carburetor with Bacardi Rum? Rowdy pondered Baines's silly suggestion and then agreed that it might work. "Bullshit," I said. "It couldn't possibly work." Rowdy grinned and reached for the bottle tucked away in a bag behind the passenger seat, explaining that if the liquid in the glass container could get us blasted, it might do well for him to give the carburetor a sip of this intoxicating spirit. Baines chuckled and gave Rowdy and me a wise-ass sort of grin. He told Rowdy to go for it as he lifted the cover off the casing that covered the carburetor inside the front of the van just below the tape deck.

Expertly Rowdy poured a slim stream of Bacardi Rum from the glass bottle into the top of the carburetor and into its guts below. He waited a few seconds, then told Baines to try to start the engine. Baines turned the key and pumped the gas pedal, and the engine weakly attempted to start; coughing and sputtering several times before it died. Rowdy poured a tad more Bacardi into the carburetor and told Baines to give more time for the alcohol to vaporize inside the carburetor. About ten seconds passed before Rowdy told Baines to try to start the van a second time.

Cough, cough. Sputter, sputter. Cough, sputter, cough, sputter, sputter, sputter, varoom, varoom, varoom. The van's engine roared as Baines floored the gas pedal for about fifteen seconds before letting up and allowing the van to continue a healthy, steady idle. Rowdy took a swig of Bacardi and handed the bottle to

Baines. Baines took a swig and offered Rowdy a high five.

I moved forward from the back of the van to snag my share of the Jamaican spirit just as Baines shouted out at the top of his lungs, "Yo ho and a bottle of rum!" We burst out in laughter and continued laughing until tears filled our eyes making it difficult to see.

Once we were out of the park, Baines pointed us west on Highway 76. North of us lay the Los Coyotes Indian Reservation. We passed through Pauma Valley and the farming town of Bonsall in route to the navy coastal town of Oceanside. Baines and Rowdy's ride proved smoother than mine as I struggled to keep my balance in the beach chair at the rear of Baines's van. When we reached our destination, I felt like I had just completed the jerky Mister Toad's Ride at Disneyland. (During this trip Rowdy and I alternated seats so that neither of us would be more bruised than the other guy.)

Upon arriving in Oceanside, we found a Motel 6 located near a small marina that included not only boating slips but also small shops and a half dozen restaurants including a Chart House. We decided to stay there because it was within walking distance of the nearest watering holes and dining establishments.

We spent most of the afternoon at the beach adjacent to the marina. We consumed can after can of ice-cold Coors Silver Bullets and ate Subway sandwiches and bags of Lays potato chips. Baines and Rowdy checked out the pretty girls on the beach as usual, and I lent them my support. After several hours of getting sunburned and cooling off in the blue Pacific, we retired several more beers in our motel room and got dressed for cocktail hour and dinner at the Chart House.

In the bar we noticed close to a dozen sailors drinking and enjoying liberty. Baines, Rowdy, and I found seats at a table that provided us a view of the boats docked alongside a wharf. But getting a waiter or waitress to serve us seemed next to impossible. I suggested I go to the bar and order drinks directly from the bartender. That way, a waiter or waitress would have to bring them to our table. I offered to buy the first round, and Baines and Rowdy stayed behind to secure our spot.

As I approached the bar, I took out a hundred-dollar bill from my wallet and stood next to a sexy young girl wearing a short cocktail dress. Casually she turned to me and noticed the C-note in my hand. She asked me what I was going to do with it, and I told her I was buying drinks for my buddies. She smiled at me, shrugged her shoulders, and turned back to the bar.

When I rejoined Baines and Rowdy, I told them about the girl who had questioned me about the money. Baines looked at me as if I was a dumb shit and asked me what I thought she was up to. Just as he said this, I saw the girl leave the bar with a sailor. I pointed her out to Rowdy and Baines, and Baines started laughing. Rowdy joined him as I sat there with "naïve" written across my face. Several other girls left the bar with sailors on their arms, too, before we were called to the dining room.

Our waiter's name was Todd. He was dressed in white shorts and a white t-shirt with a Chart House logo emblazoned across the right shoulder of the t-shirt in wavy blue letters. He had straw-blond surfer hair and a bronze tan typical of table jockeys who work in most Southern California coastal town restaurants. When I asked him what his ambition was besides being a waiter, he informed us he was attending Cal State San Marcos, which lay inland in the town of the same name. He said he was majoring in kinesiology and planned to be a P.E. teacher and a high school volleyball coach.

Each of us went for the surf and turf combo. Rowdy ordered sautéed scampi and grilled filet mignon, and Baines and I opted for pan-seared scallops with New York strip steaks. I ordered potatoes au gratin, and Rowdy and Baines opted for twice-stuffed baked potatoes. Caesar salads and Tanqueray on the rocks with a twist preceded our entrees.

Over dinner we talked about our trip and then touched on our dislike for President George H.W. Bush. Baines noticed that Todd was leaning our way each time H.W.'s name was mentioned, and we decided to screw with him and praise the president against our grain. Each time Todd was within ear shot, one of us would utter a word or two about H.W., or something having to do with the federal government. *Best president ever. A true genius. John Sununu's buddy. More honorable than Ronald Reagan. The NRA. Democrats suck. Our Secret Service training. Aviator during World War II. Director of the CIA. Air Force One. The Pentagon. Barbara Bush. Camp David. Kennebunkport, Maine.* We drove the kid crazy as he tried to serve other customers and eavesdrop on our conversation at the same time. Several times Baines would start to say something and then whisper with his hand cupped to hide his mouth.

Finally, Todd could not take it anymore. He approached us and excitedly whispered, "Do you gentlemen work for the State Department?"

Rowdy leaned over to him and whispered emphatically, "We sure as hell do!"

Todd grinned, and as he backed away said, "I thought so!" We continued our charade through dessert, which was New York cheesecake topped with a raspberry compote for each of us. We gladly washed down our sweets with Irish coffees lightly topped with mint-flavored whipped cream.

After an exceptional dinner and leaving a big tip, we bid a proud Todd good-bye. As we walked through the Chart House bar, we noticed that several of the girls who had left with sailors earlier were back with the intention of putting their hooks into other suspecting customers. When we returned to our motel room, we polished off the remaining dark Bacardi Rum as we watched the late night news and then reruns of *Leave It to Beaver.*

The next morning, Baines walked to a nearby auto parts shop. When he returned, he sprayed the carburetor of his Chevy van with STP carburetor cleaner and poured a six-ounce can of STP fuel additive into the van's gas tank. Needless to say, Baines's engine fired up without a cough or sputter and let us know that it was time for us to get on the road to home.

CHAPTER 37

The Red Ball

Baines wrote many short stories. My favorite is titled *The Red Ball*. I found it in a manila folder Tim Ball gave me the day we salvaged things from Baines's condominium.

The Red Ball

A frigid swell of power thrust upon the top of his bare head. He surged on. An icy penetration numbed the glossed cheeks. His head, while cold, bore no resemblance to the torso. The lower section, clothed in wool, endured in a state of comfortable and cozy warmth. A fervent feeling on the bottom, in contrast to a piercing state on the top genuinely reflected his constitution. Parallel, a placid atmosphere merged with an urge to get the hell inside before he froze his balls off.

He ceased jogging and leaned against a streetsign post. Catching his breath, he took in the environs. The 5:00a.m. sun prepared to enlighten the city below which housed all the minions that, along with Coy Diamond, would soon embark outward from a domin ad emerge as trembling throngs. As the surrounding reality engulfed Coy, a blurring car zoomed past with high speed. A sportscar—perhaps a Porsche or a Triumph. He glanced at his watch, still glowing in the dark, and resumed his running.

He gazed at the black sky. The clarity produced a vigor which instigated a love of life and humanity. He flashed around a corner and felt a splotch of something cool and moist on his right hand. He instantly recognized a bird had released itself while both flew down the street.

"Oh glory be," thought Coy, "a sumptuous way to begin the day—nature's beauty has crapped upon my hand. Oh thank you, God."

Not to be distracted by trivialities, Coy maintained the course down the empty hillside street. He thought he heard a loud noise coming from around the bend. Maybe an accident. Quite possibly an accident. Yes, very definitely an accident. An accident—the car that whizzed by moments ago. He huffed and puffed. He must reach his destination before the fatigue floors him.

He arrived at a mailbox post that looked as if a locomotive flattened it...No car!

"This must have been the noise," he said loudly to himself, "where the hell---." To his left, down an immense dark gully, an overturned small car reclined with its wheels still spinning.

Fright stung his body. Speechless, he panicked. He tripped over the mailbox remains. He picked himself up and tripped again. He twisted his head around for help. A dark empty silence enveloped the atmosphere, which in turn, enshrined his body in total desolate isolation. This aloneness produced an urgency for Coy to grasp the situation and thrust it into his own hands. He gulped and leaned his head downward into the lurid gully.

"Hello." He shouted, "hello there! Are you alright?" Silence answered him.

He possessed a perpetual aversion to blood—even his own. He gulped and cleared his throat.

He cautiously placed his foot on the descending path to the overturned automobile. The wheels seemed passive and flagging now, but nevertheless still revolving. Coy's heartbeat tripled its pace causing the pulse in his neck to create an exploding perception.

"Ohhhh," a groan from the car.

"Alive," said Coy. "Hello, are you alright? Don't worry."

"Ohhhh," the groan again. The steep gully looked to be approximately fifteen feet deep.

"Ahh, I'm coming," comforted Coy.

The early morning breeze pierced his sweaty brow and created a chill. He shivered and sucked in the moisture from his upper lip. Precariously, he worked his way deeper and deeper. Despite a jogging avocation, a clumsy, but well-meaning, figure descended to the depths of this gully. The dirt clogged his tennis shoes. Each step caused additional soil to enter. His feet submerged into the spongy marshy dirt.

Finally, five feet from the bottom, he slipped on his rear-end and slid the rest of the way. Now a slovenly piece of disorder, he picked himself up and felt a gigantic mud stain on his buttocks cling to his cheeks. His once bright crimson sweatsuit appeared two-toned brown and red.

He approached and the motionless wheels glared at him. He knocked on the passenger door. No answer.

"Hello!" He vainly attempted to peer underneath.
The small car, being a convertible, trapped the person—
or the remains—beneath. He frantically strutted around
the wreck searching for wedges to see through.

"Ohhh," the groan once again.

"You're alive. Thank god, you're alive!" he yelled.

He huffed and puffed and then ventured to actually
move he car. Although small, it may as well have weighed
100,000 pounds. He twisted his head searching for a
house with a light. No houses, let alone lights.

"Get me out of here," shouted a distinctly female
voice.

Coy leaped toward the car. I'm trying, I'm trying.
Are you hurt?

"I'm not hurt, I'm stuck. Get me out!" replied the
voice.

The voice sounded youngish—maybe 25 or so.

"You're not hurt?"

"No goddamnit. I'm still in my seatbelt. I feel a little
funny, but I don' hurt," she answered.

"Probably in shock," he thought. "On the other
hand, it could me a miracle from heaven or something.
She sounds pretty too."

"Don't you know how lucky you are?" he said to her.

"Lucky? How would you like to be stuck in this
stinking driver's seat? Who the hell are you anyway?"

"I'm just a local jogger. I heard your crash and here
I am," he replied.

"Heard the crash, huh? Well listen Mr. Jogger, why
don't you get your running ass in gear and find someone
to get me out of this stupid position, OK?"

From this, Coy mused what a pesky young thing
she sounded like. An active tongue combined with good

looks. In addition, he figured <u>she</u> was in no position to give <u>him</u> orders.

"You're right, I'll go and try to find someone," he said.

"Goddamn," he thought, "I wish I could lift that car. I'd turn that lousy thing over and see a beautiful girl sitting in the driver's seat. Then I'd get in the passenger's side and she'd drive us away to some beach retreat, and then wham bam. Of course, if she kept up this foul-mouth routine, I could keep her strapped in the seat and plug her here."

With this splendid array of fantasy, Coy realized a surge of power rage through his body. He picked up an old beer can and daringly twisted it so that it came apart.

"Yeah, I'll find you some help alright1" he shouted at the top of his lungs.

He thrust his arms underneath the car. It refused to budge.

"Hey, what are you doin' buster?" she cried.

"Shut up in there, will ya'," blurted Coy.

"What a ya trying to do, lift the car? Listen you lame-brain, go get some help."

"Shut up!" screamed Coy.

Oblivious to her plea, he huffed and puffed and strained every solitary muscle in his trendy trim, but noticeably awkward, body. The perspiration streamed his now gaunt face. He distinguished colors of reds and yellows and greens. His consciousness veered to a nullity of strange satisfaction.

Coy conquered the dynamics of mass and gravity. "I'm doing it, I'm doing it!" he yelled. The car gradually moved its way to the conventional everyday exposure. The incessant breathing persisted. Thanks to the daring Coy, the car made it—up and over it rolled—and unscathed too. Coy felt simultaneous nausea and ecstasy.

Revulsion took over when he perceived a nebulous vision in the driver's seat. He rubbed his eyes in disbelief. In the seat, curled into a solid red ball, squatted the parts of Coy's visionary energy.

"Jesus Christ, what the hell is that?"

His heart stood in his mouth. He shook and trembled. His eyes sprung into terror as the red ball sprouted ears. Then a nose. Arms. Legs.

"Where's the face...the face?" he screamed in terror. "What do you want? I'm sorry. I swear I am!" He attempted to run up the bank of the gully but stark fright kept him frozen. He could not keep his eyes off the red glow.

The red ball illuminated the entire gully. It stretched its legs and looked as if it desired to leap from the seat. Then it paused and appeared unwilling to relinquish the seat. It took on a protective air.

Coy's tenuous state caused immobility. A kind of paralysis enveloped him and he stood at attention glaring at this horrific crimson reality.

Then, without notice, the red ball leaped at him with the speed of some type of dangerous canker. To his dismay, Coy dodged the intruder.

"Leave me alone. I'm OK! I swear I am."

The red ball with legs like bright red stakes in the ground, stood erect right next to him. A head with no eyes seemed to blast through Coy's face. His entire body reeked of dust and filth and desiccation.

Coy, preparing to faint, saw the huge red ears that seemed to grow. In fact, the entire red mass expanded and soared to a height of ten or more feet. Coy gazed up at the faceless wonder. The surrounding reality ceased to exist. He cocked his head upward and channeled his vision in the direction of the miraculous apparition.

"Don't hurt me, oh please don't hurt me!" he pleaded. "I didn't mean to disturb you, honest."

One of the red legs kneed Coy in the crotch.

"Ohhh," he groaned in agony.

The ground around him shook as he stood frozen in despair. He wanted to run but remained glued to the dissolving ground. It emerged as a sloppy, marshy, and dank soil. Coy progressively sunk. Down...down. His speech flew away. The muted and paralyzed body plunged to the depths.

For added measure, the long leg of the glowing ball slammed its foot on top of Coy's bare head. Nothing remained. Sealed forever.

Later that morning, when the sun reached its peak of penetrating and lustful fervor, the police discovered a dead, but limp, body of a 30ish male. At the outset, they noticed the bizarre position and location of the corpse; the sweatsuit-clad body straddled both seats of a late model sports car situated in a deep gully. The car, in perfect condition, seemed out-of-place—so did its occupant.

Baines told me the gist of the story after he wrote it and indicated that when he read it to his classmates in Wally Graves's creative writing class, his classmates praised him for his creativity and wanted to know the symbolism of the red ball in his story. He told me he responded with the following typical Baines Spivington colloquialism, "The red ball does not mean jack shit!"

CHAPTER 38

A Few Other Classic Experiences with My Friend, Baines Spivington

Years ago Baines Spivington wanted to buy an Alpha Romeo convertible sports car. His mother told him she would provide him with some of the money to do so. She gave him a check for $10,000 and told him to cash it at the local Bank of America branch. There, the teller and then the bank manager told Baines his mother's check needed a day to clear before he could cash it. Baines was frustrated, because he had made an appointment that same day to purchase the car, and that same day he was leaving with me on a trip to Davis, California, to visit our friend Rowdy, who was teaching summer school at UC Davis.

Not willing to give up easily, Baines called the dealership and explained his dilemma to his salesman. Without hesitation the salesman asked Baines if he had credit cards, and Baines replied he had several. He asked Baines if he had received credit card checks through the mail recently, and Baines confirmed he had.

He told Baines he would accept the credit card checks in full payment for Baines's new vehicle.

Excited and relieved, we raced down the San Diego Freeway in my car to a dealership in Palos Verdes (I cannot recall the name of the place). Baines had a big grin on his face as he greeted the salesman upon our arrival. He filled out and signed four credit card checks at a bit over $5,000 a piece. He turned them over to his savior, who ushered us into the financial manager's office to finalize the paperwork. When we left the dealership and headed north on the 405 Freeway toward Davis, California, Baines was a happy owner of a brand-spanking-new, black Alpha Romeo convertible sports car.

Baines had always been a late morning sleeper. Before he lived in his condo, he lived in an apartment next door to an Armstrong Nursery on Magnolia Boulevard in Sherman Oaks. Every morning he was awakened by the noise of a delivery truck, the sound of a leaf blower revving full blast, or the sound of a forklift stacking pallets high with various garden materials. Every once in a while on a Saturday, I would go out to dinner with Baines or have take-out with him at his place. I would stay over at his apartment, and we would watch movies, sporting events, or reruns of shows such as *Mash*, *Seinfeld*, or *Leave It to Beaver*. On the following Sunday morning, I shared his frustration by being awakened by the noise generated by the nursery next door.

One Saturday Baines called me at my Simi Valley home and asked that I do him a favor. Although I was not staying at his place that evening, he asked if I could call the nursery the next morning and say that I was a neighbor who had been awakened by the noise coming from their business. He said he would call me first to tell me whether a delivery truck, blower, or forklift would be the subject of my complaint. No problem I said, and I told Baines I'd be waiting for his call the next morning.

At 7:00 a.m. my phone rang, waking me from a deep sleep. A cursing Baines told me several delivery trucks had caused him frustration and that he had called to register his own complaint already. He gave me the nursery's number and asked me to call him after I called the nursery.

I dialed the number, and when a female voice on the other end of the line answered "Armstrong Nursery" and asked what I needed, I complained, as Baines had, that delivery trucks in their yard had awakend me and that I was tired of this continuing nuisance. Calmly, she explained that she did not know how this was possible, because I was calling from area code 805 according to their phone system, and their area code was 818. Stunned and dumbfounded, I didn't know what to say and hung up the phone. I called Baines and told him what had happened. Without laughing he responded that he would have to depend on Rowdy the next time, because he lived in the same 818 area code as he did. Even with Rowdy's help and the help of others he recruited, Baines continued to lose early morning sleep until he moved into a condominium.

Baines Spivington was always a neat freak. Everything had its place—in his car, in his bedroom at his parents' house, in his apartment, or in his condominium. One day when visiting Baines at his condo, I noticed in the building's elevator that the emblem of the manufacturer, Otis Elevator Company, had black marker graffiti scarring its surface. I mentioned this to Baines, who agreed that the graffiti needed to be removed.

I visited several more times without Baines taking any action to remove the graffiti. Finally, when an old lady riding with me pointed to the black mess and wondered aloud what SOB had done it, I again mentioned it to Baines. We were going out to dinner that night at the Mikado, and Baines decided that when we returned, the elevator mess would be taken care of once and for all.

As usual we had a few beers before we took off for the Mikado. We then took surface streets the whole way to the restaurant, because time was on our side, and we were in no rush. Dickens Avenue served as our route much of the way. Baines took it to avoid certain types of black and white vehicles.

We both had our standard Tanqueray martinis on the rocks with a twist as we pondered the menu before ordering. We both chose boat dinners, which included soup, salad, teriyaki chicken and beef, and vegetable and shrimp tempura. We also ordered two large hot sakes.

As we continued to sip away at our martinis, we talked about how each time we dined at the Mikado, the decor and architecture inside was different. The location of the sushi bar had crisscrossed the restaurant many times over the years, and the seating had changed many times too; we'd gone from sitting cross-legged at short tables in bamboo booths to sitting in overstuffed cloth chairs that pushed halfway under normal-size bamboo tables. The only thing constant over the years was the location of the kitchen, which was entered and exited through two flapping hardwood doors.

Over dinner we talked about the serious task ahead of us—getting rid of the graffiti on the Otis Elevator Company emblem. Being a schoolteacher, I was aware of graffiti-removal techniques used by custodians at the various schools where I'd taught. I suggested to Baines that Aqua Net hair spray was a popular way of ridding metal of black marker graffiti. The spray and a paper towel or cotton cloth towel were all one needed to do the job. Baines did not have Aqua Net, he said, but did have Consort hair spray for men. Over a second sake and green tea ice cream for dessert, we further contemplated the grueling task ahead of us.

We took Dickens Avenue back to Baines's condo complex and arrived just around 10:00 p.m. Baines found the Consort where he had last used it—on the counter in the main bathroom. He grabbed a cotton cloth from a junk drawer in the kitchen. We were both ready and poised to restore the dignity of the Otis Elevator Company emblem. Baines was to be the sprayer, and I was to be the wiper. Also, to keep the elevator stationary at one floor, Baines needed to keep his finger on the third-floor button, thus hopefully preventing another resident or visitor from interrupting us during our restoration effort.

In the elevator we calmly positioned ourselves. We were ready to take on the graffiti. Baines pressed the button on top of the Consort, and a stream of hair spray shot out from the can and onto the scarred elevator emblem. The graffiti started to drip immediately, and we started to feel we were going to win this challenge. I encouraged Baines to shoot a second stream of spray before I attacked the dripping surface with the cotton cloth. He did this with vigor and a sense of power before I told him to stop. I leaned forward and forcefully wiped the cloth across the area, right to left and back, several times where Baines had sprayed. And then a sudden sense of shock shot through my body. I backed away from my work, and Baines and I stared in disbelief at the results of our efforts. Not only was the graffiti gone from the emblem; the Otis Elevator Company emblem was gone as well.

The spray had acted as a solvent on not only the black markings but also the emblem, which apparently was made of plastic. Baines and I quickly exited our work site and bolted for his condo door which we closed behind us

The next week the service man for the Otis Elevator Company appeared to do some minor maintenance. He replaced the missing emblem with one made of brass.

Working at Ralphs Supermarket at times could be more fun than work. The time I spent working the night crew stocking shelves with Baines was no exception. Usually before the store closed and work was to ensue, Baines would make an announcement on the PA that customers should come forward for a final checkout at the register. He did this regularly because the PA was situated on the liquor department counter where he worked.

One night when it was near closing time, Baines announced over the PA that there were a few remaining breaded chicken lips on sale in the meat department. I was bagging groceries for an elderly lady as he made the announcement, and as I started to laugh, she kindly asked if I would go to the meat department and bring her the remaining lips. I pretended to go to the meat department and then returned to tell her they were sold out.

Another night, Baines had just closed the front sliding glass door when a man outside started pounding on it demanding that he be allowed to come into the store to make several last minute purchases. Baines was ready to kick the pounder's ass until he recognized through the glass that it was none other than George C. Scott, the actor. Baines opened the door, invited him in, shook his hand, and asked him what he needed. "Booze, son, plenty of booze," he growled in reply. He told Baines he was going to a big party in nearby Toluca Lake.

Baines wheeled a shopping cart down the liquor aisle as George C. filled it—Bacardi and Coca-Cola; Dewar's Scotch; three bottles of chilled Moët champagne; Schweppes ginger ale; two bottles of Cutty Sark Scotch; Jim Beam Bourbon; Smirnoff Vodka; Southern Comfort; Jose Cuervo Tequila; Triple Sec; Cointreau; Schweppes Collins Mix; Schweppes Tonic Mix.

As Baines rang up the order on the liquor register, he chitchatted with the gravelly voiced actor, praising him for his famous early role as General "Buck" Turgidson in the 1964 film *Dr. Strangelove.* "Buck" rewarded Baines with a $50 tip as he counted his change from the second of two $100 bills. I helped George C. Scott to his car with the cart of booze, and he rewarded me with $5 for my efforts.

One December night, when Baines and I had gotten off work at 12:00 a.m. and sucked down a pitcher of beer at Little Tony's Pizzeria, Baines saw a need for a Christmas tree. He was planning to have a holiday party in the large room just off from the garage and his bedroom at La Casa de la Puerta Roja. Ralphs was selling trees off its back lot, and at night there was no security. Baines knew that trying to lift one of the trees off the lot might be risky. But the beers gave us the confidence that we could pull it off. Like clockwork, in Baines's '57 Chevy, we slowly approached the tree lot from an alley behind Ralphs and Pep Boys. When Baines eased his car to a quiet stop, I leaped out of the car, opened its right rear door, and grabbed the nearest tree I could get hold of, and threw it across the backseat and closed the door. With me back in the front passenger's seat, Baines burned rubber out of the lot without anyone seeing us commit our petty theft.

The party was two nights later. One of the late arrivals was Cleo Gardner, an older box boy who had been newly assigned to do security that night and the night before at the Ralphs Christmas tree lot. As he slowly sipped on an eggnog in a snow-covered glass, he commented to Baines that he sure had a beautiful Christmas tree.

Baines responded with a grin, "Thanks, Cleo. You know, my tree is almost as beautiful as the one's you guard at the Ralphs Christmas tree lot."

CHAPTER 39

A Few Last Words about My Friend, Baines Spivington

The last time I saw Baines Spivington in person was at the seashore of Hollywood Beach, California. It was early November on a sunny Sunday afternoon. He had spent part of a long weekend with me at my mobile home. During the days we lounged on the beach enjoying an Indian summer. At night we barbecued and drank beer and watched sports and movies on TV, much as we did at his condo in Sherman Oaks. On that Sunday afternoon, he suggested that we go to a movie. I told him that it being such a nice day, I wished to surf fish and enjoy soaking rays while sitting in my beach chair. He seemed a bit upset that I did not feel like joining him for one of his favorite pastimes. He didn't leave pissed off, but he did not attempt to ask me a second time to join him.

I did not talk to Baines for quite a while. The last time I spoke to him was the night I called him to ask about the film *Meet John Doe*.

Baines had not hung out with our friend Rowdy Ralphs for quite a long time. Rowdy had married Carrie Ann, and she had given birth to their lovely son, whom they named Davis. Not too long before the condominium fire took Baines's life, Rowdy and Baines had re-upped their relationship. They had begun to go here and there together—to movies, museums, and an occasional lunch. They had plans to see one another on a more regular basis.

During the last few years of Baines's life, he had a girlfriend he cared a great deal for. He wined and dined her and chauffeured her to and from the airport when she left to travel or visit relatives or returned to LA. When she was in town, he was not lonely. When she wasn't in town, Baines was lonely.

When Isabel Schwartz died, Baines was crushed. When Ethan Schwartz died, Baines was totally lost. The security Baines felt when his mother and stepfather were alive was gone. My wife, Rowdy Ralphs, and I recognized the physical exhaustion and mental anguish Baines went through when he took on the overwhelmingly challenging job of being executor of his stepfather's estate. I don't think members of his family knew the pain Baines went through by having to sell Ethan's house, pay off debts, and distribute remaining money to those relatives designated in his will.

When Ethan was alive, he and Baines made regular visits to the same psychiatrist. When Ethan died, Baines continued to visit the psychiatrist, who prescribed a drug for Baines to keep him on an even keel. He suffered from an anxiety disorder, and Klonopin worked wonders for him. He no longer feared going to the bank to sign deposit slips and withdrawal slips as he had in the past when his hand would shake so hard he could not legibly write his name; the magic antidote not only gave him the confidence to carry out these tasks, but also enabled him to live a fairly normal everyday life. Instead of calling me and telling me he had to cancel a dinner date with Debi and me at our home because of his fear of driving, he confidently drove himself out to Simi Valley to enjoy one of Debi's gourmet meals.

Before the fire, Baines seemed to be living a life that mattered.

Epilogue

After I finished writing about my friend, Baines Spivington, I decided that I would offer to share his story with several of his relatives. His brother-in-law and sisters welcomed the opportunity to read about him, because they did not know much about his life except for what they had observed during an occasional social and family gathering. Baines's sisters were much older than their brother and were basically out of the house and on their own when he was still a kid.

After agreeing to accept a copy of my manuscript, his brother-in-law cleared the air about several issues I had questions about. One was why I had not been invited to participate in the spreading of my friend's ashes in the Pacific Ocean? The other, the cause of the fire?

Baines's brother-in-law was not up front with me when he shared Baines's ashes were put to rest at sea. My friend's body was kept in the morgue while the authorities continued to try to determine what had caused the fire. I am not sure whether they eventually did spread his ashes, and I did not ask.

The cause of the fire was basically undetermined according to Baines's brother-in-law, although the authorities speculated that the cause might have had something to do with wiring. It took six months to repair the condominium and sell it.

Although my friend of forty years is physically gone, he remains alive in my mind and in *Forty Crazy Years of Friendship.*